First World War
and Army of Occupation
War Diary
France, Belgium and Germany

5 CAVALRY DIVISION
Divisional Troops
5 Signal Squadron
1 January 1917 - 30 March 1918

WO95/1163/4

The Naval & Military Press Ltd
www.nmarchive.com
Published in association with The National Archives

Published by

The Naval & Military Press Ltd

Unit 10 Ridgewood Industrial Park,

Uckfield, East Sussex,

TN22 5QE England

Tel: +44 (0) 1825 749494

www.naval-military-press.com

www.nmarchive.com

This diary has been reprinted in facsimile from the original. Any imperfections are inevitably reproduced and the quality may fall short of modern type and cartographic standards.

© **Crown Copyright**
Images reproduced by permission of The National Archives, London, England, 2015.

Contents

Document type	Place/Title	Date From	Date To
Heading	WO95/1163/4		
Heading	5 Cav Div Troops 5 Signal SQ 1917 Jan-1918 Mar		
Heading	War Diary of 5th Signal Squadron. From 1st January 1917. To 31st January 1917		
War Diary	Dargnies	01/01/1917	31/01/1917
Diagram etc	Message Chart-January 1917.		
War Diary	Dargnies	01/02/1917	24/02/1917
Diagram etc	Message Chart-February 1917		
War Diary	Dargnies.	01/03/1917	20/03/1917
War Diary	Senarpont	20/03/1917	21/03/1917
War Diary	Pont-De-Metz	21/03/1917	21/03/1917
War Diary	Dargnies	21/03/1917	21/03/1917
War Diary	Pont-De-Metz	21/03/1917	22/03/1917
War Diary	Cerisy	22/03/1917	23/03/1917
War Diary	Pont-De-Metz	23/03/1917	23/03/1917
War Diary	Peronne	24/03/1917	27/03/1917
War Diary	Templeux	27/03/1917	27/03/1917
War Diary	Peronne	28/03/1917	30/03/1917
War Diary	Villers-Bretonneux	30/03/1917	31/03/1917
Operation(al) Order(s)	Appendix 2 5th Signal Squadron Operation Order No. 20	21/03/1917	21/03/1917
Operation(al) Order(s)	Appendix 1 5th Signal Squadron Operation Order No. 19	19/03/1917	19/03/1917
Diagram etc	Appendix 3 Communications-5th. Cavalry Division. 25/3/17.		
Diagram etc	Communications-5th Cavalry Division. 31-3-17. Appendix 4		
Diagram etc	Message Chart For March 1917. Appendix 6		
War Diary	Villers-Bretonneux.	01/04/1917	14/04/1917
War Diary	Guizancourt	14/04/1917	30/04/1917
Operation(al) Order(s)	Appendix 1 5th Squadron Operation Order No. 22	11/04/1917	11/04/1917
Diagram etc	Appendix 2 Diagram Of Communication 5th Cavalry Division 30-4-1917		
Diagram etc	Message Chart For April 1917. Appendix 3		
War Diary	Guizancourt.	01/05/1917	15/05/1917
War Diary	Nobescourt Farm	15/05/1917	31/05/1917
Diagram etc	Appendix 1 5th Cavalry Division Communications 9.0 am 16-5-1917		
Diagram etc	Appendix 2 5th Cavalry Division Communications 9.0 am 19-5-1917		
Diagram etc	Appendix 3 5th Cavalry Division Communications 9.0 a.m. 24-5-1917		
Diagram etc	5th Cavalry Division Communications 9.0 a.m. 31-5-1917. Appendix 4		
Diagram etc	Message Chart 1st-15th May Appendix 5		
Diagram etc	Message Chart For Period 23rd-31st May.		
Diagram etc	Message Chart For Week Ending 22/5/17		
War Diary	Nobescourt Farm	01/06/1917	30/06/1917
Diagram etc	Appendix 1 Communications-5th Cavalry Division 30-6-17		

Diagram etc	Appendix 2 Messages Chart-June 1917		
War Diary	Nobescourt Farm	01/07/1917	10/07/1917
War Diary	Bouvincourt	10/07/1917	10/07/1917
War Diary	Nobescourt Fm.	10/07/1917	10/07/1917
War Diary	Bouvincourt	10/07/1917	16/07/1917
War Diary	Treux	16/07/1917	16/07/1917
War Diary	St Pol	16/07/1917	31/07/1917
War Diary	Heuchin	31/07/1917	31/07/1917
Diagram etc	Appendix 1 Communications-5th Cavalry Division 10-7-1917		
Operation(al) Order(s)	Appendix 2 5th Signal Squadron Operation Order No. 23.	13/07/1917	13/07/1917
Diagram etc	Communications 5th Cavalry Division 18-7-1917. Appendix 3		
Diagram etc	Communications 5th Cavalry Division 23-7-1917 Appendix 4		
Diagram etc	Communications 5th Cavalry Division 31-7-1917. Appendix 5		
Diagram etc	Message Chart July. 1917. Appendix 6		
War Diary	Heuchin	01/08/1917	31/08/1917
Diagram etc	5th Signal Squadron Circuit Diagram. 31-8-17		
Diagram etc	August 1917 Telegrams. & D.R.L.S. Packet Chart		
War Diary	Heuchin	01/09/1917	30/09/1917
Diagram etc	Map. Len. 11 Scale 1/100,000		
Diagram etc	September 1917 Telegram & D.A.L.S. Packet Chart.		
War Diary	Heuchin	01/10/1917	06/10/1917
War Diary	Steenbecque	06/10/1917	11/10/1917
War Diary	Poperinghe	14/10/1917	14/10/1917
War Diary	Renescure	15/10/1917	15/10/1917
War Diary	Fressin	16/10/1917	01/11/1917
Diagram etc	Communications.-5th. Cavalry Division 14th October 1917.		
Diagram etc	5th Signal Squadron Circuit Diagram 12.10.1917		
Diagram etc	Communications-5th Cavalry Division Night 15th/16th October 1917.		
Diagram etc	Diagram Of 5th Cavalry Division Communications		
Miscellaneous	Operation Orders by Capt. C. L. Andrews Cmdg. 5th Signal Sqdn.	13/10/1917	13/10/1917
Operation(al) Order(s)	5th Signal Squadron Operation Order No. 25		
Diagram etc	October-1917. Telegram & D.R.L.S. Packet Chart.		
War Diary	Fressin	07/11/1917	10/11/1917
War Diary	Occoches	10/11/1917	11/11/1917
War Diary	Querrieu	11/11/1917	11/11/1917
War Diary	Bouvincourt	12/11/1917	20/11/1917
War Diary	Fins R 9 B 8. 8. (ref map 57 c)	20/11/1917	20/11/1917
War Diary	Equancourt.	22/11/1917	22/11/1917
War Diary	Suzanne	23/11/1917	27/11/1917
War Diary	Monchy-Lagache	27/11/1917	30/11/1917
War Diary	Ref 62 C. E 5 A.	30/11/1917	30/11/1917
Diagram etc	5th Signal Squadron Diagram Of Communications		
Diagram etc	Circuit Diagram of 5th Cav. Div. Communications		
Diagram etc	Diagram of Communications 5th Cavalry Division.		
Diagram etc	Diagram of Communications 5th Cavalry Division		
Diagram etc	Circuit Diagram of 5th Cav. Div Communications		
Diagram etc	5th Cavalry Division Circuit Diagram.		
War Diary	E 5 A 50 ref. map 62 C 1/40000	30/11/1917	02/12/1917

War Diary	Heudicourt	02/12/1917	03/12/1917
War Diary	Longavesne	03/12/1917	08/12/1917
War Diary	Monchy-Lagache.	08/12/1917	23/12/1917
Diagram etc	5th Signal Squadron Circuit Diagram		
Diagram etc	5th Signal Squadron Circuit Diagram.		
Diagram etc	5th Signal Squadron Circuit Diagram		
War Diary	Monchy Lagache	01/01/1918	27/01/1918
War Diary	Bouvincourt	27/01/1918	31/01/1918
Diagram etc	Appendix 1 Communications-5th Cavalry Division 1st January 1918		
Diagram etc	Appendix 2 Communications-Dismounted Divisions & 5th Cavalry Division 31-1-18.		
War Diary	Bouvincourt	01/02/1918	17/02/1918
War Diary	Pont De Metz	17/02/1918	20/03/1918
War Diary	Marseilles.	30/03/1918	30/03/1918

WO 95/1163/4

5. Signal Sqdn

5 CAV DIV TROOPS

5 SIGNAL SQ.

1917 JAN — 1918 MAR

SERIAL NO. 749.

Confidential

War Diary

of

5th SIGNAL SQUADRON.

FROM 1st January 1917. 1917 TO 31st January 1917. 191

WAR DIARY of 5th Signal Squadron 5th Cavalry Division
or
INTELLIGENCE SUMMARY Vol VII

Army Form C. 2118.

(Erase heading not required.)

Hour, Date, Place	Summary of Events and Information	Remarks and references to Appendices
1/1/17 – 31/1/17 DARANIES	Squadron in permanent billets. Communications same as for December 1916. Moveable sheet attached.	Appendix 1

Adcivers Capt.
O.C. 5th Signal Squadron

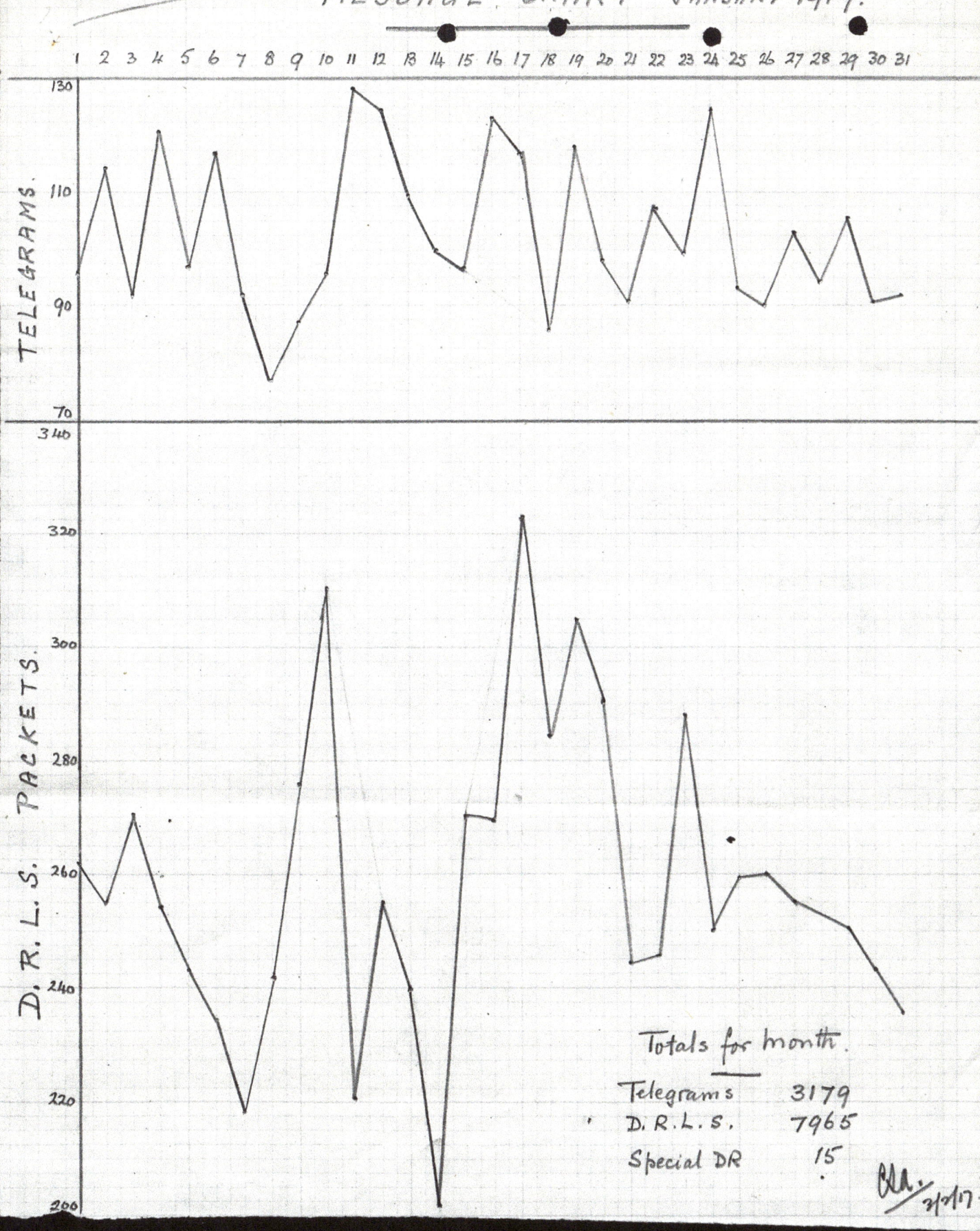

Vol VIII
5th Signal Squadron
Army Form C. 2118.

WAR DIARY
or
INTELLIGENCE SUMMARY

(Erase heading not required.)

Instructions regarding War Diaries and Intelligence Summaries are contained in F.S. Regs., Part II. and the Staff Manual respectively. Title pages will be prepared in manuscript.

Hour, Date, Place	Summary of Events and Information	Remarks and references to Appendices
1/2/17 DARANIES	Squadron in permanent billets. Telephonic communication established with 5th Cavalry supply column at MERS	(RS.)
17/2/17 DARANIES	"F" Pack wireless section joined Squadron from Cavalry Corps	(R.)
24/2/17 "	Signals detachment R.F.C. Liaison Officer joined Squadron	(R.)
24/2/17	R.F.C. detachment joined squadron. Diagram of communications as for last month. Message chart for month attached.	(R.) Appendix 1

W Reynard Capt
Commanding 5th Signal Squadron

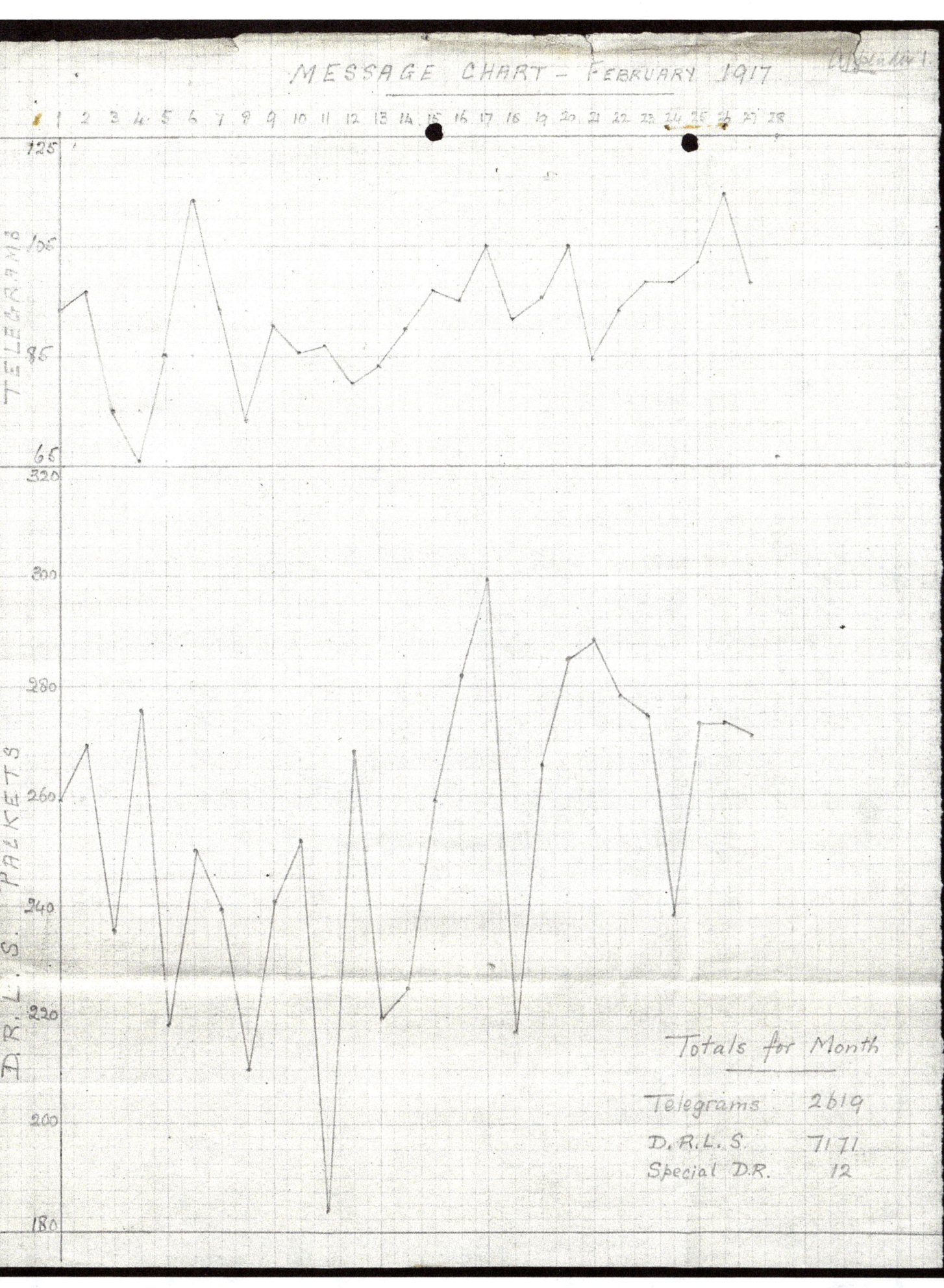

Army Form C. 2118.

WAR DIARY of 5th Signal Squadron
INTELLIGENCE SUMMARY March 1917 Vol IX

(Erase heading not required.)

Instructions regarding War Diaries and Intelligence Summaries are contained in F.S. Regs., Part II. and the Staff Manual respectively. Title pages will be prepared in manuscript.

Hour, Date, Place	Summary of Events and Information	Remarks and references to Appendices
1/3/17 – 11/3/17 DARGNIES.	Squadron in permanent billets. Communications as for February.	OAA
12/3/17 DARGNIES.	Orders received from Division to be prepared to move at 48 hours notice.	5th Can Div. No. GA 529 OAA
7am 19/3/17 DARGNIES	Warning notice received from Division to march on 20th.	
11.45 am " "	Telephonic communication with 17th Bde. R.H.A. on leave.	
1.0 pm " "	" " Canadian Cav. Bde.	
" "	Communication with Canadian Cav. Bde. (BEAMP (FOUCAUCOURT)) and 17th Bde. R.H.A. (RAMBURES) maintained by despatch rider.	
10.15 pm " "	Operation Order received from Division for march eastwards on 20th; despatched to all units by Special DR	
11.0 pm " "	Operation Order No. 19 issued by OC 5th Signal Squadron to march.	Appendix 1. OAA
8.30 am 20/3/17 DARGNIES	Telegraphic Telephonic communication with Ambala discontinued. Brigade ceased.	
9.0 am " "	Squadron (less Advanced Rear Report Centre) marched to SENARPONT.	
9.30 am " "	Advanced Report Centre left for SENARPONT	
10.45 am " SENARPONT	Advanced Report Centre established	
12.15 pm " "	Telephonic communication established with Rear Report Centre through	
12.45 pm " "	ARSEVILLE. Squadron arrived. Communication with Brigade & Divnl Troops by despatch rider.	
1.0 pm " "	Operation Orders received from Rear Report Centre for continuance of march eastwards on 21st.	OAA

1247 W 3299 200,000 (E) 8/14 J.B.C. & A. Forms/C. 2118/11.

Army Form C. 2118.

WAR DIARY
INTELLIGENCE SUMMARY
(Erase heading not required.)

Instructions regarding War Diaries and Intelligence Summaries are contained in F. S. Regs., Part II. and the Staff Manual respectively. Title pages will be prepared in manuscript.

Hour, Date, Place		Summary of Events and Information	Remarks and references to Appendices
8.30 am 21/3/17	SENARPONT	Advanced Report Centre left for PONT-DE-METZ	
9.30 am	"	Squadron marched to PONT-DE-METZ	
10.45 am	PONT-DE-METZ	Advanced Report Centre arrived	
11.30 am	"	Telephonic communication established with Fourth Army via AMIENS Civil Exchange.	
12 noon	DARNIES	Divisional Report Centre closed.	
"	PONT-DE-METZ	" " opened; telegraphic work circulating via AMIENS Military Office.	
12.30 pm	"	General Staff put on the telephone.	
3.50 pm	"	Operation Orders received & despatched to all units by Special D.R.	
4.0 pm	"	Lines laid to A.S.O.1's billet and Q office	
5.0 pm	"	Communication to all units of Division by DR. Operation Order No. 20 received by the 5th Signal Squadron for Lunch.	Appendix 2.
8.15 am 22/3/17	PONT-DE-METZ	Squadron marched to CERISY.	
8.45 am	"	Advanced Report Centre left for CERISY.	
10.15 am	CERISY	Advanced Report Centre arrived	
12 noon	"	Telephonic communication established with Fourth Army being through CERISY Exchange	
12.30 pm	"	Operation Orders received from Rear Report Centre telegraphed to all units.	
2 pm	"	Squadron arrived.	

Army Form C. 2118.

WAR DIARY
or
INTELLIGENCE SUMMARY

(Erase heading not required.)

Instructions regarding War Diaries and Intelligence Summaries are contained in F. S. Regs., Part II. and the Staff Manual respectively. Title pages will be prepared in manuscript.

3.

Hour, Date, Place		Summary of Events and Information	Remarks and references to Appendices
12.30 am 23/3/17	CERISY	Operation Orders received from Rear Report Centre & dispatched to all units.	
9.0 am	"	Advanced Report Centre CERISY CHÂTEAU marched to PERONNE; 2 SPs left Report Centre closed 1pm	
9.45 am	PONT-DE-METZ	Rear Report Centre arrived.	
12 noon	PERONNE	Advanced Report Centre arrived.	
2 pm	"	Signal Office opened. Squadron arrived. Line from Fourth Army Ltd in.	
3.30 pm	"	Line through to General Staffs	
4.45 pm	"	Telegraphic telephonic communication established with Fourth Army.	
6.0 pm	"	Operation Orders received & dispatched to all units.	
8.30 pm	"	Wireless Station near FAUBOURG DE PARIS connected by telephone.	
7.0 am 24/3/17	PERONNE	Message dropping ground for aeroplanes established to high ground near West of PERONNE, & connected by telephone to Signal Office.	
9.0 am	"	Line through to 15th Corps H.A. Exchange.	
9.30 am	"	Visual station established at MONT ST. QUENTIN	
10.25 am	"	Visual station observed Canadian Bde. entering MOISLAINS, but could not attract their attention	
1.55 pm	"	Visual communication established with Canadian Bde. at MOISLAINS Visual station in telephonic communication with Signal Office by telephone or line being laid to Canadian Bde.	
6.3 pm	"	"Q" Branch connected by telephone.	
6.0 pm	"	Canadian Bde. at MOISLAINS connected by telephone.	
7.0 pm	"	Australian Bde. at ESTRÉES-EN-CHAUSSÉE connected by telephone	
9.40 pm	"	Visual Station at MONT-ST-QUENTIN closed down.	
11.0 pm	"	Operation Orders received & dispatched to all units by D.R. Time advanced 1 hour i.e. to midnight, to bring in "Summer Time"	DrA

1247. W 3259 200,000 (E) 8/14 J.B.C. & A. Forms/C. 2118/11.

Army Form C. 2118.

'WAR' DIARY
INTELLIGENCE SUMMARY

(Erase heading not required.)

Instructions regarding War Diaries and Intelligence Summaries are contained in F.S. Regs., Part II. and the Staff Manual respectively. Title pages will be prepared in manuscript.

Hour, Date, Place	Summary of Events and Information	Remarks and references to Appendices
25/3/17 PERONNE	Telegraphic communication with Australian & Canadian Bdes. as well as telephone. Cyclist Relay Post established to connect to Secunderabad Bde.	
9.10pm 25/3/17 "	R.A.C. message dropping Cuclist out from 7am to 7pm. Operation orders received & despatched to all units by D.R.	Ra.
26/3/17 PERONNE	No change in communications. During to rain wires to Brigade too bad to work sounder; changed to vibrator.	Ra.
12.45pm 27/3/17 PERONNE	Secunderabad Bde. moved to bivouac north of HALLE; communication still maintained by cyclist D.R.	
2.30pm " "	Advanced Report Centre left for TEMPLEUX-LA-FOSSE.	
4.0pm " "	Advanced Report Centre established in church at TEMPLEUX-LA-FOSSE; telephonic communication with Rear Report Centre at PERONNE.	
4.30pm TEMPLEUX	Visual station from Advanced Report Centre established N.E. of TEMPLEUX-LA-FOSSE.	
4.45pm " "	Visual communication established with Australian Bde. at Bois de TINCOURT	
5.10pm " "	" " " " Canadian Bde. at LIERAMONT.	Ra.
7.30pm " "	Communication to both brigades also by mounted D.R.	
28/3/17 PERONNE	Advanced Report Centre closed returned to PERONNE.	
3pm " "	Communications as on morning of 27th.	
6pm " "	Secunderabad Bde. moved to bivouac N. of CLERY.	Ra.
" "	Operation orders received & despatched to all units by D.R.	
9am 29/3/17 PERONNE	Canadian Bde. Report Centre closed at MUISLAINS, telephonic communication ceased.	
11.10am " "	Australian Bde. Report Centre closed at ESTREE, telephonic communication ceased. Communication with all units of Division by D.R. Australian Bde. moved to CAPPY; Australian Bde. to Bois de MEREAUCOURT.	Ra.

Army Form C. 2118.

WAR DIARY
or
INTELLIGENCE SUMMARY

(Erase heading not required.)

No. 5.

Instructions regarding War Diaries and Intelligence Summaries are contained in F. S. Regs., Part II. and the Staff Manual respectively. Title pages will be prepared in manuscript.

Hour, Date, Place	Summary of Events and Information	Remarks and references to Appendices
1.0 am 30/3/17 PERONNE.	Operation orders received & despatched to all units by D.R.	
10.0 am " "	Advanced Report Centre left for VILLERS-BRETONNEUX.	
10.15 am " "	Squadron marched to VILLERS-BRETONNEUX.	
12.40 pm " VILLERS-BRETONNEUX	Advanced Report Centre arrived	
2.0 pm " "	Report Centre closed at PERONNE & opened at VILLERS-BRETONNEUX. Communication with Fourth Army through III Corps Signals Sub-Office	
5.15 pm " "	Direct line through to Fourth Army.	
5.45 pm " "	General Staff & A.S.O.1 connected by telephone. Communication by telephone with Canadian Bde. at CAPPY.	Ack.
8.30 pm " "	Communication by telephone with Secunderabad Bde. at BAYON VILLERS	
9.30 pm " "	Telegraphic communication with Canadian Bde.	
9.0 am 31/3/17 VILLERS-BRETONNEUX	Q Branch, O.C. A.S.C. & D.A.D.O.S. connected by telephone	Ack.
10.0 am " "	Communication by telephone & telegraph with Australia Bde. at WARFUSÉE. Communication with receiving units by D.R.	
" "	Diagram & communication at PERONNE attached	Appendix 3.
" "	" VILLERS-BRETONNEUX attached	" 4
" "	Message chart for month attached	" 5

M. Reynal Capt.
O.C. 5th Signal Squadron

5th Signal Squadron   Appendix 2

Operation Order No.20

21/3/17

Ref. 1/100,000 maps.

1. The Squadron will march to-morrow to CERISY forming up with Divnl. Hdqrs. at the Church ~~Place~~ PONT-DE-METZ at 8.15 am.
Route will be via LONGEAU and VILLERS BRETONNEUX.

2. Cpt. Andrews   Advanced Report Centre, as per margin,
Cpl. Clover   will march at 9.0 am to CERISY, and
Spr. Rattenbury will open up there at 12 noon
4 Motor Cyclists

3. Main Report Centre (remaining motor cyclists + 3 telephone operators) will remain at PONT-DE-METZ until further orders.

4. In future on conclusion of a march Sgt. Atkinson will report whether all motor cyclists are in, Cpl. Kirk will do the same as regards linemen + operators, L/Cpl. Bray as regards pigeoneers.

A. Andrews
Capt.
5th Signal Squadron

5th Signal Squadron Appendix 681
Operation Order No. 19

Ref. 1/100,000 maps.   19/3/17

1. The Division is marching to-morrow to the
   HORNOY area.

2. <u>The Squadron</u> (less Advanced + Rear Report Centres)
Mounted ⎫ will march to-morrow to SENARPONT, parading
Men   ⎬ at 9.0 a.m. with head of column at cross-roads
Wireless ⎪ Eastern exit of DARGNIES, in order of march
Transport⎭ as per margin.
          Cyclists will parade at same hour but will
          march independently to SENARPONT under Cpl. Kirk

3.   All wagons will be loaded by 8.0 a.m.

4.   <u>Advanced Report Centre</u>, as per margin, will
Capt Andrews⎫ parade outside Signal office at 9.30 a.m., +
Cpl. Clover ⎬ open at SENARPONT at 11.0 a.m.
Spr. Rattenbury⎪
4 M.C. DRs ⎭

5.   <u>Rear Report Centre</u>, will remain at DARGNIES
      until further orders.

Issued at 11pm.   A Andrews
                                      Capt
                                   5th Signal Squadron

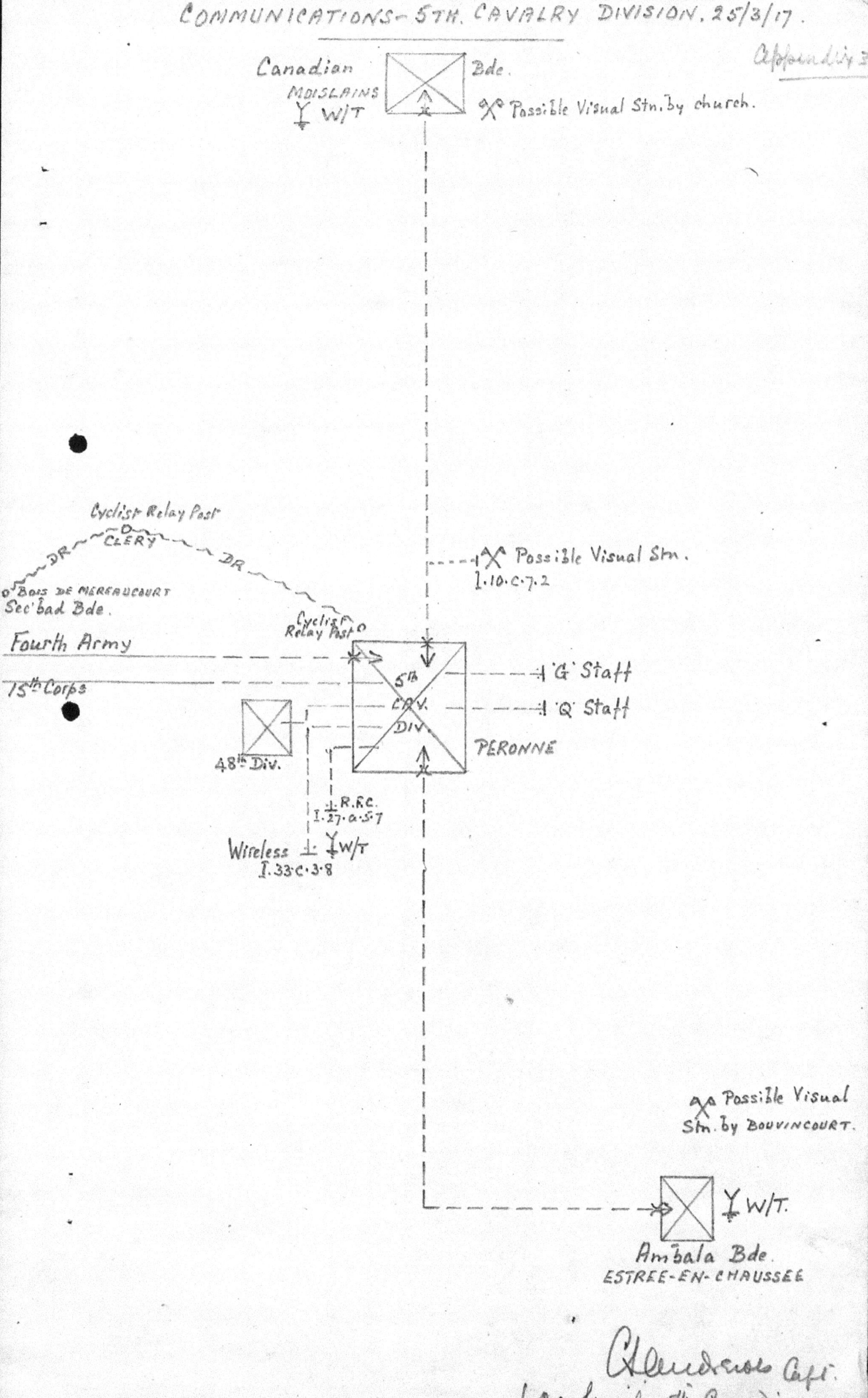

Appendix 4.

Communications - 5TH CAVALRY DIVISION.
31 - 3 - 17.

```
                                    CANADIAN
                                    CAV. BDE.
                                    ────────
                                    |   X   |
                                    |   ↗   |
                                    ─────────
                                    CAPPY
                                       │
                                       │
                                       │
                    AMBALA CAV. BDE.   │
                    ────────           │
                    |   X  |           │
                    |  ↗   |           │
                    ────────           │
                    WARFUSEE           │
                       │               │
                       │     SEC'BAD CAV. BDE.
                       │     ────────
                       │     |   X   |
                       │     |   ↗   |
                       │     ─────────
                       │     BAYONVILLERS
                       │       │
To Fourth Army →  ─────────────┤
                  |  ↗  ↓  ↗  |
                  |     X     |
                  ─────────────
                  5TH. CAV. DIV.
                  VILLERS-BRETONNEUX
                  │ │ │ │ │ │
```

'G' Staff
G. S.O.2.
'Q' Branch
O.C. A.S.C.
D.A.D.D.S.
O.C. Signals
Signals Mess

W Reynolds. Capt.
O.C. Signals, 5th Cav. Div.
31/3/17.

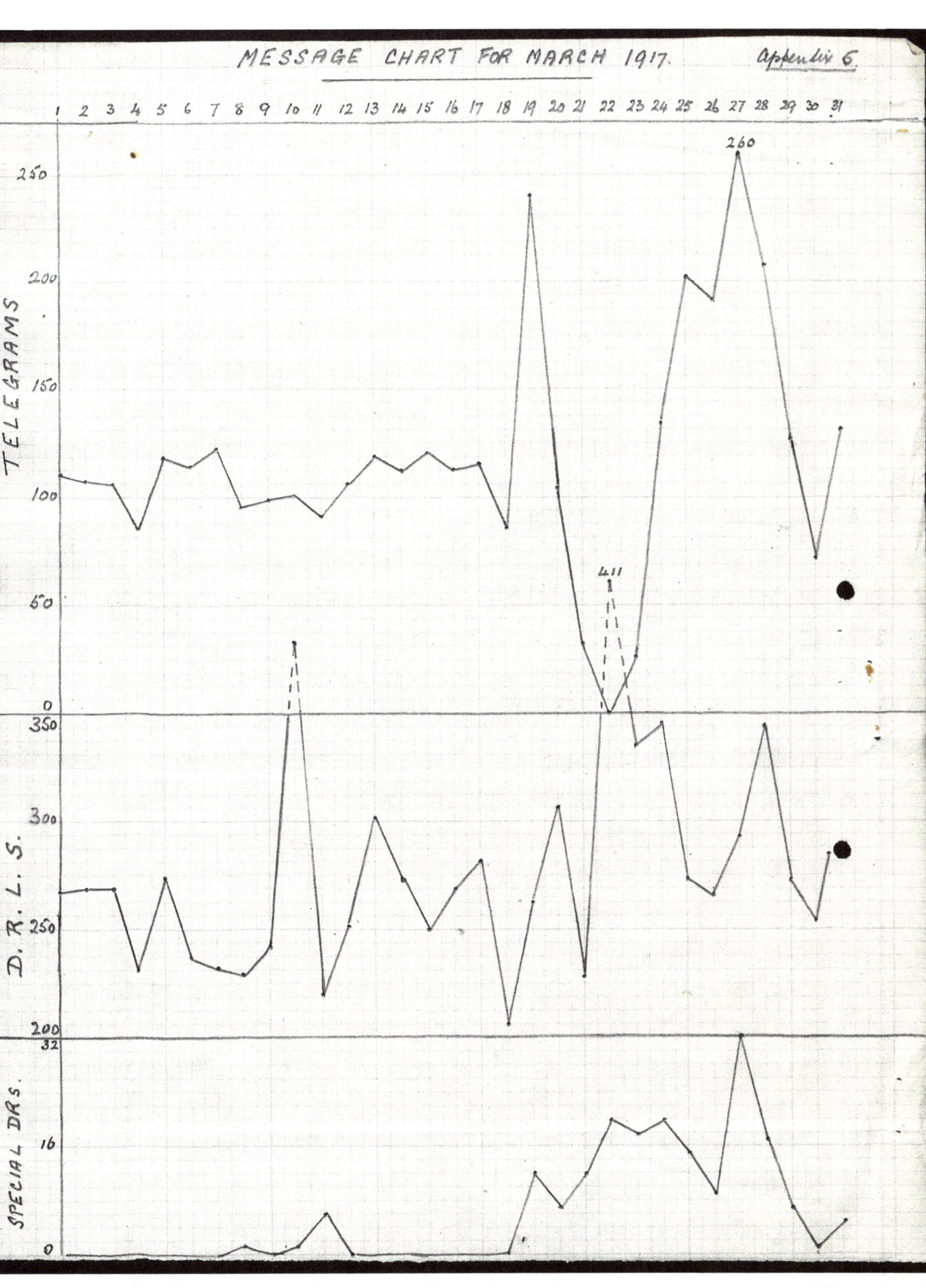

Vol IX
Army Form C. 2118.

5th Signal Squadron
April 1917.

WAR DIARY
or
INTELLIGENCE SUMMARY
(Erase heading not required.)

Hour, Date, Place	Summary of Events and Information	Remarks and references to Appendices
1/4/17 – 10/4/17 VILLERS-BRETONNEUX	Squadron in billets at VILLERS-BRETONNEUX. Communications as at end of march.	—
5pm 11/4/17 VILLERS-BRETONNEUX	Operation Orders received to march on 12th to TERTRY. Squadron Operation Order No 2 issued to march to TERTRY	Appendix 1.
6pm " "	Orders received from Division cancelling move for 12th, to be prepared to move on 13th on receipt of orders	—
10.30pm " "	Operation Orders issued for Squadron to act on Operation Order No 2	—
5pm 13/4/17 " "	Verbal Orders received for march on 14th to GUIZANCOURT, embussing at GUIZANCOURT to TERTRY.	—
7.45am 14/4/17 VILLERS-BRETONNEUX	Squadron marched to GUIZANCOURT	—
9.0am " " GUIZANCOURT	Advanced Report Centre left for GUIZANCOURT	
1.30am " " "	Advanced Report Centre arrived & set up Signal Office	
1.30pm " " "	"G" Staff connected to Exchange	
3.0pm " " VILLERS-BRETONNEUX	Rear Report Centre closed	
3.10pm " " GUIZANCOURT	Telephonic communication established with Parulli Bgnd at VILLERS CARBONNEL.	
2.0pm " " "	Squadron arrived	
" " " "	17th Brigade R.H.A. connected to Exchange	
5.0pm " " "	Reinforcements connected to Exchange	—

Army Form C. 2118.

WAR DIARY or INTELLIGENCE SUMMARY
(Erase heading not required.)

Instructions regarding War Diaries and Intelligence Summaries are contained in F. S. Regs., Part II. and the Staff Manual respectively. Title pages will be prepared in manuscript.

Hour, Date, Place	Summary of Events and Information	Remarks and references to Appendices
9.15am 15/4/17 GUIZANCOURT	Telephonic communication established with Reconnoitred Car Bde at TREFCON.	
1.30pm " "	Telephonic communication established with Australia Bde at PAULAINCOURT	
3.30pm " "	R.T.C. Report Centre connected to Exchange; also R Branch	
16/4/17 GUIZANCOURT	5th Cav. Supply Column connected to IV Corps Exchange at MASNIL	
17/4/17 GUIZANCOURT	also D.C. A.S.C. connected to Exchange	
7.20pm 20/4/17 GUIZANCOURT	Telephonic communication established with Canadian Cav. Bde	
6.00pm 21/4/17 GUIZANCOURT	accompanied no 9 Sqdn R.F.C. connected to 4 Urgent Limber Exchange	
9.0 am 22/4/17 GUIZANCOURT	Working Party left to clean up lines in back area	
7pm 25/4/17 GUIZANCOURT	Working Party returned from cleaning up lines in back area	
30/4/17 GUIZANCOURT	Communications as per diagram attached. Message chart for month attached.	Appendix 2 Appendix 3

Alexandrew Capt.
O.C. 5th Signal Squadron

Appendix 70

5th Signal Squadron
Operation Order No. 22.
11th April 1917

Reference: 1/40,000 BAPAUME & ST QUENTIN Maps.

1. Divisional Headquarters is to-day, to move from ATHIES to TERTRY.

2. The Squadron, less Advanced & Rear Report Centres will parade outside the Signal Office at 7 a.m., under Lieut. JONES.

3. Advanced Report Centre, as per margin, will
   (margin: Lieut. Mathews, Cpl Clover, 6 Motor Cyclists, Cpl. Raine & Side Car, Spr. Battenburg)
   open outside the Signal Office at 9.0 a.m., proceeding via POEUILLY – BRAY – ESTREES – CO – CHAUSSÉE to TERTRY, arriving at dest. between 11 a.m. & 12 noon.

4. Rear Report Centre, as per margin, will remain
   (margin: Sgt. Atkinson, 2 Motor Cyclists, Spr. Jones)
   here until 3 p.m., & will then close down, & proceed direct to TERTRY.

5. The Cyclists will parade at 8.0 a.m. under Cpl. Kirk, & proceed direct to TERTRY on the same road as Advanced Report Centre.

War Diary.

H. Saunders
Capt.
5th Signal Squadron

Appendix 2

DIAGRAM OF COMMUNICATION
5TH CAVALRY DIVISION
30-4-1917

Ambala Cav Bde
Caulaincourt

Secunderabad Cav Bde
Tretcon.

Canadian Cav Bde

5TH Cav. Div
GUIZANCOURT

'G' 5/H
'Q'
O.C. A.S.C.
17th Bde. R.H.A.
R.F.C. Report Centre.
Signals Mess.

IVTH ARMY
Villers Carbonnel

VIITH Corps
NESTLE

5TH Cav Supply Column
Herly

A. W. Dresser Capt
OC Signals Sqn
5th Cav. Div.

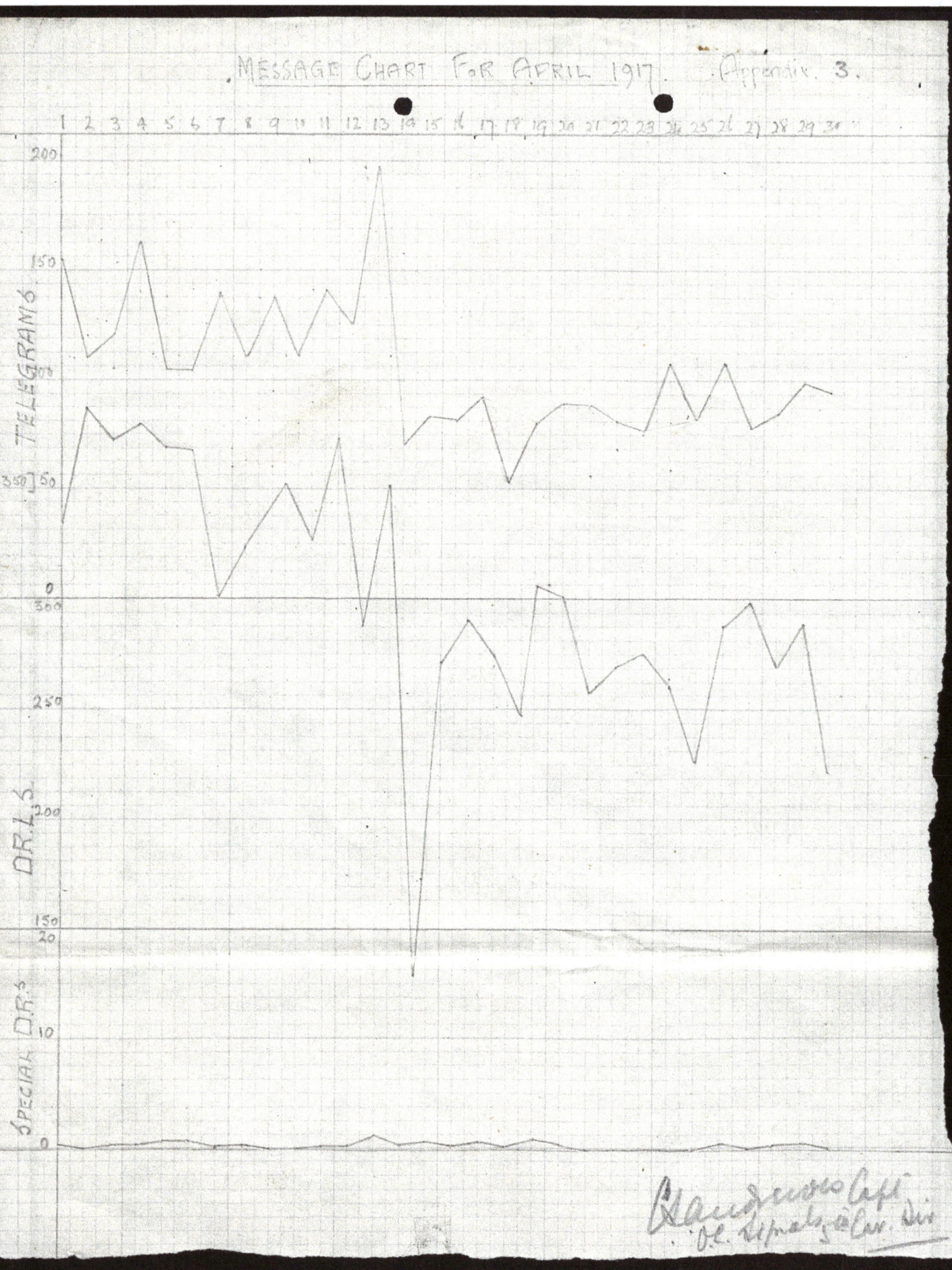

WAR DIARY or INTELLIGENCE SUMMARY

(Erase heading not required.)

Army Form C. 2118.

5th Signal Squadron
1 May 1917
Vol. IX

Instructions regarding War Diaries and Intelligence Summaries are contained in F.S. Regs., Part II. and the Staff Manual respectively. Title pages will be prepared in manuscript.

Hour, Date, Place	Summary of Events and Information	Remarks and references to Appendices
1/5/17 GUIZANCOURT	Squadron in temporary billets. Communications as at end of April.	Nil.
4/5/17 GUIZANCOURT	Air-line laid to Canadian Cav. Bde. (ATHIES) to replace cable.	Nil.
5/5/17 GUIZANCOURT	Air-line laid to Secunderabad Cav. Bde. (TREFCON) to replace cable.	Nil.
11/5/17 GUIZANCOURT	Instructions received from Division that we are taking over front of Sqn. Division.	Nil.
14/5/17 GUIZANCOURT	Party sent to MOISECOURT FARM to set up Signal Office. Canadian Cav. Bde. Signal Office closed at ATHIES and re-opened at VERMAND.	Nil.
9.30am 15/5/17 GUIZANCOURT	Squadron left for MOISECOURT FARM.	
4.30pm 15/5/17 MOISECOURT FARM	Signal Office opened. Telephonic communication with Sqth Division at BOUVINCOURT. Following local connections made to Exchange — 'G' Staff, 'Q' Staff, G.S.O.(I), O.C. A.S.C., R.A. Exchange Office closed down at GUIZANCOURT at 5pm.	
9am 16/5/17 MOISECOURT FARM	Telephonic communication with — 176th Inf. Bde. (ROISEL), Secunderabad Cav. Bde. (MONTIGNY FARM), 35th Division (BEAUVOIS). 5th Cavalry Division took over Command from Sqth Division. Communications as per attached diagram	Appendix 1 Nil.
9am 19/5/17 MOISECOURT FARM	Cavalry Corps took over from III Corps. Communications now as per attached diagram.	Appendix 2 Nil.

Army Form C. 2118.

WAR DIARY or INTELLIGENCE SUMMARY

(Erase heading not required.)

Hour, Date, Place	Summary of Events and Information	Remarks and references to Appendices
20/5/17 NOISESCOURT FARM	87th French Division took over from 35th Division at BEAUVOIS; telephonic communication through 59th Division.	QQ.
21/5/17 NOBESCOURT FARM	No. 52 Section T'Battery Anti-Aircraft connected to Exchange.	QQ.
23/5/17 NOBESCOURT FARM	Air Line laid to Canadian Cav. Bde. (YADENCOURT) to replace cable	QQ.
24/5/17 NOBESCOURT FARM	4th Cavalry Division (HERVILLY) took over from 176th Inf. Bde. Communication at 9am as per diagram attached.	Appendix 3. QQ.
25/5/17 NOBESCOURT FARM	Supply Column (MONCHY LAGACHE) connected to Amiens Cav. Bde. Exchange (CAULAINCOURT)	QQ.
27/5/17 NOBESCOURT FARM	59th Division left area. Direct telephonic communication with 87th Division (French)	QQ.
29/5/17 NOBESCOURT FARM	No. 4 Section 160th Tunnelling Coy. (VENDELLES) connected to Exchange. Communication as per attached diagram	Appendix 4
31/5/17 NOBESCOURT FARM	Heaviest traffic during any one day was on May 22nd when 364 telegrams and 423 sealed packets were disposed of. Message sheets for month attached	Appendix 5

[signed] Raymond Carl Sydon
Captain
5th Signal Sqdn

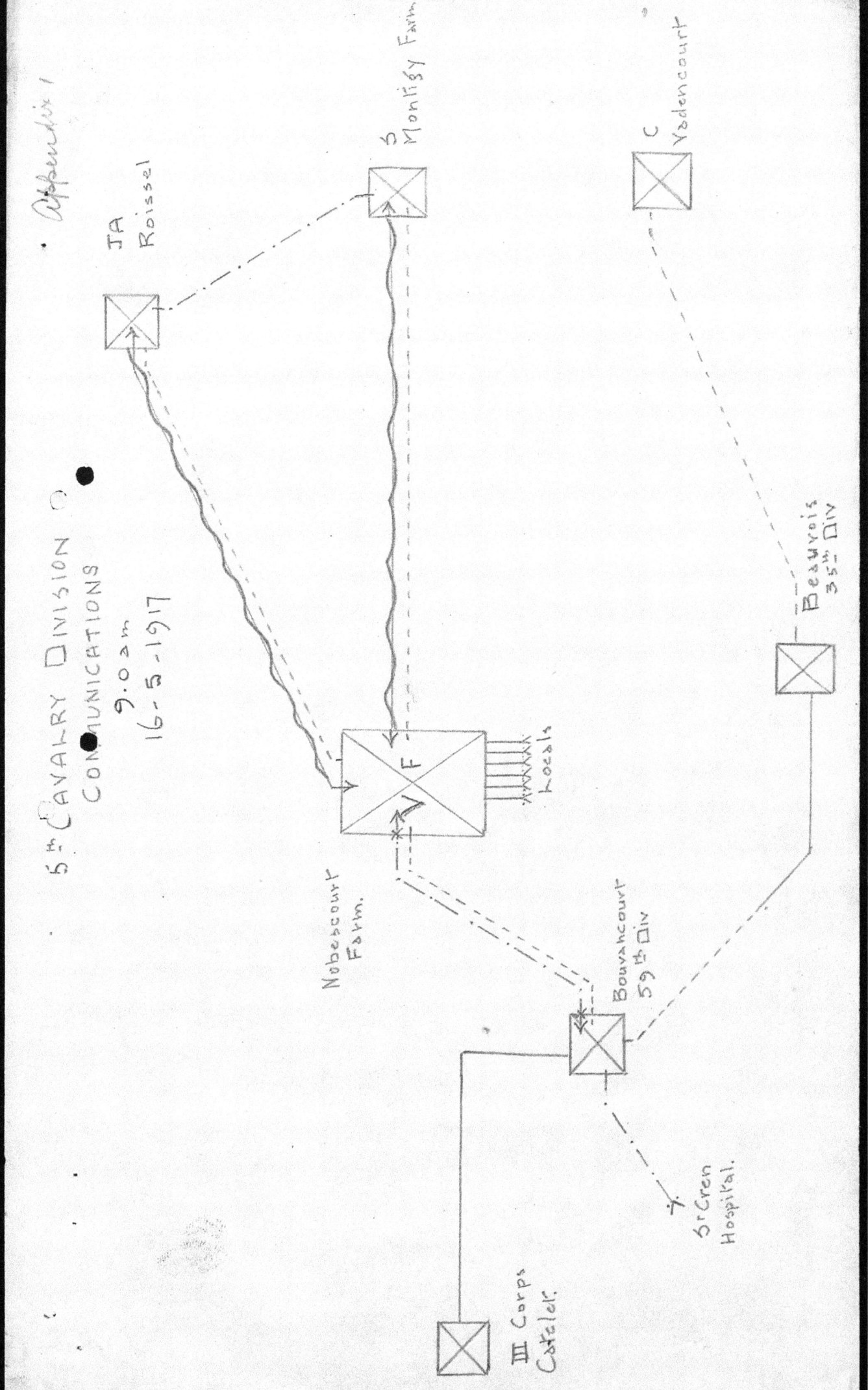

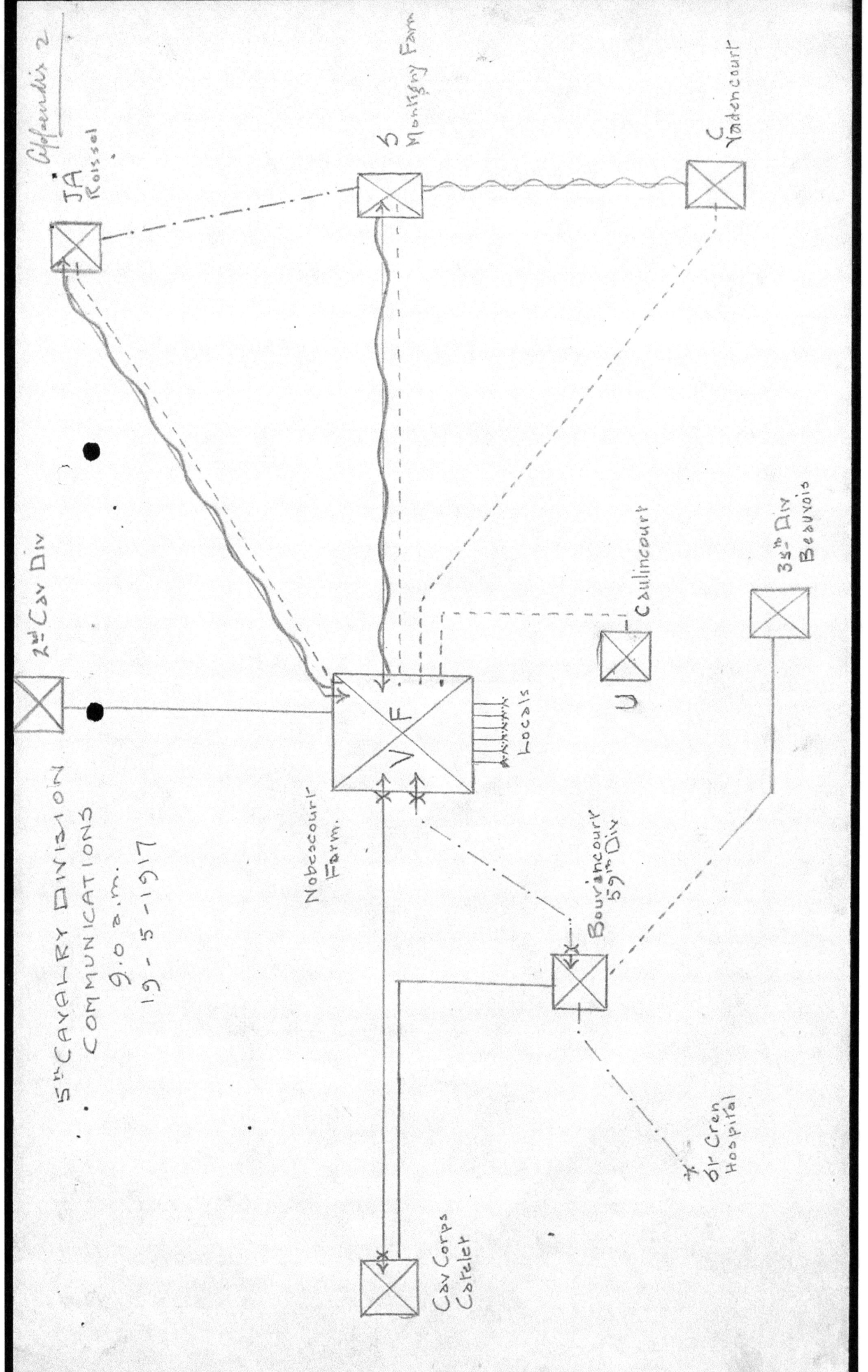

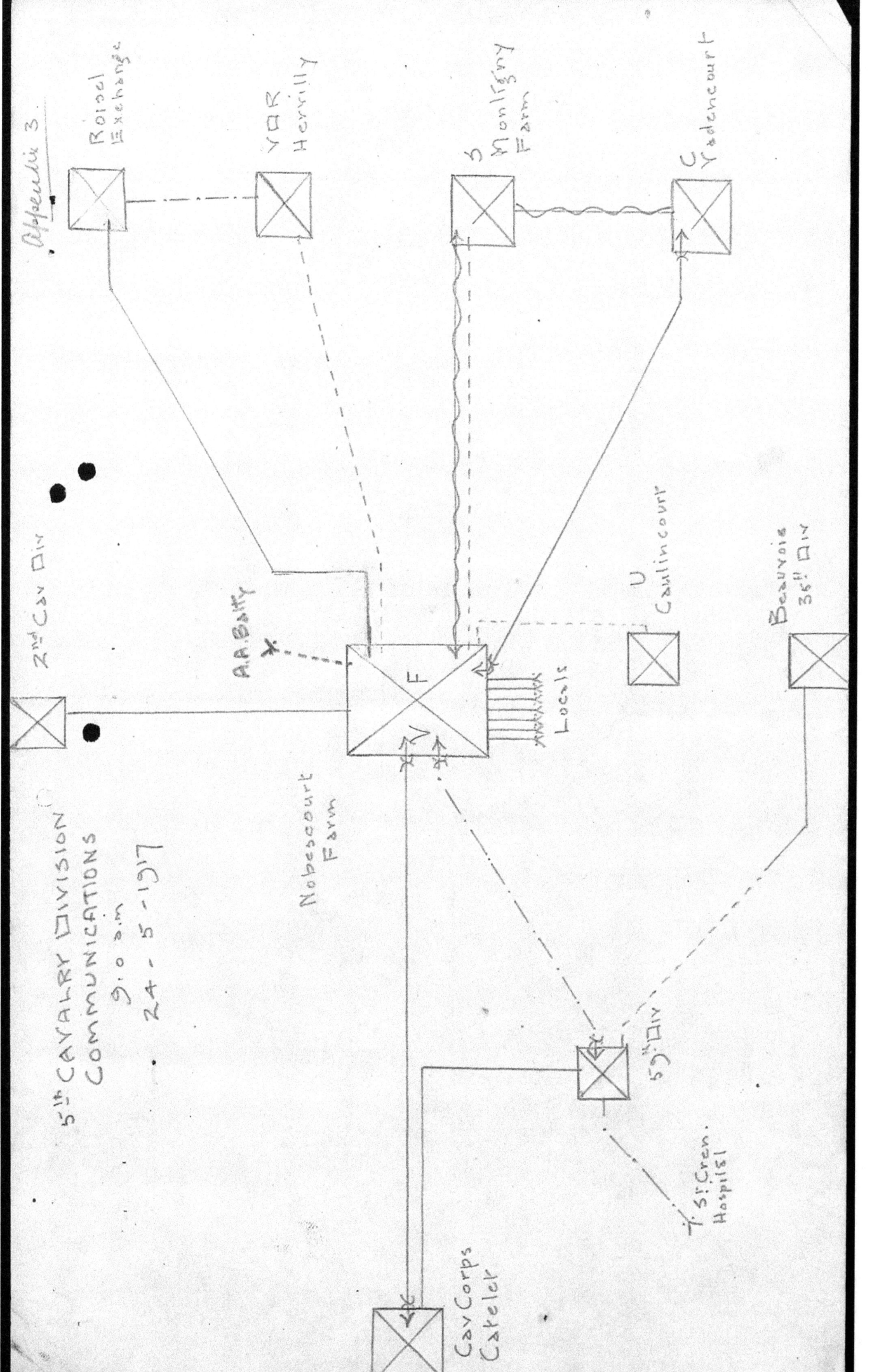

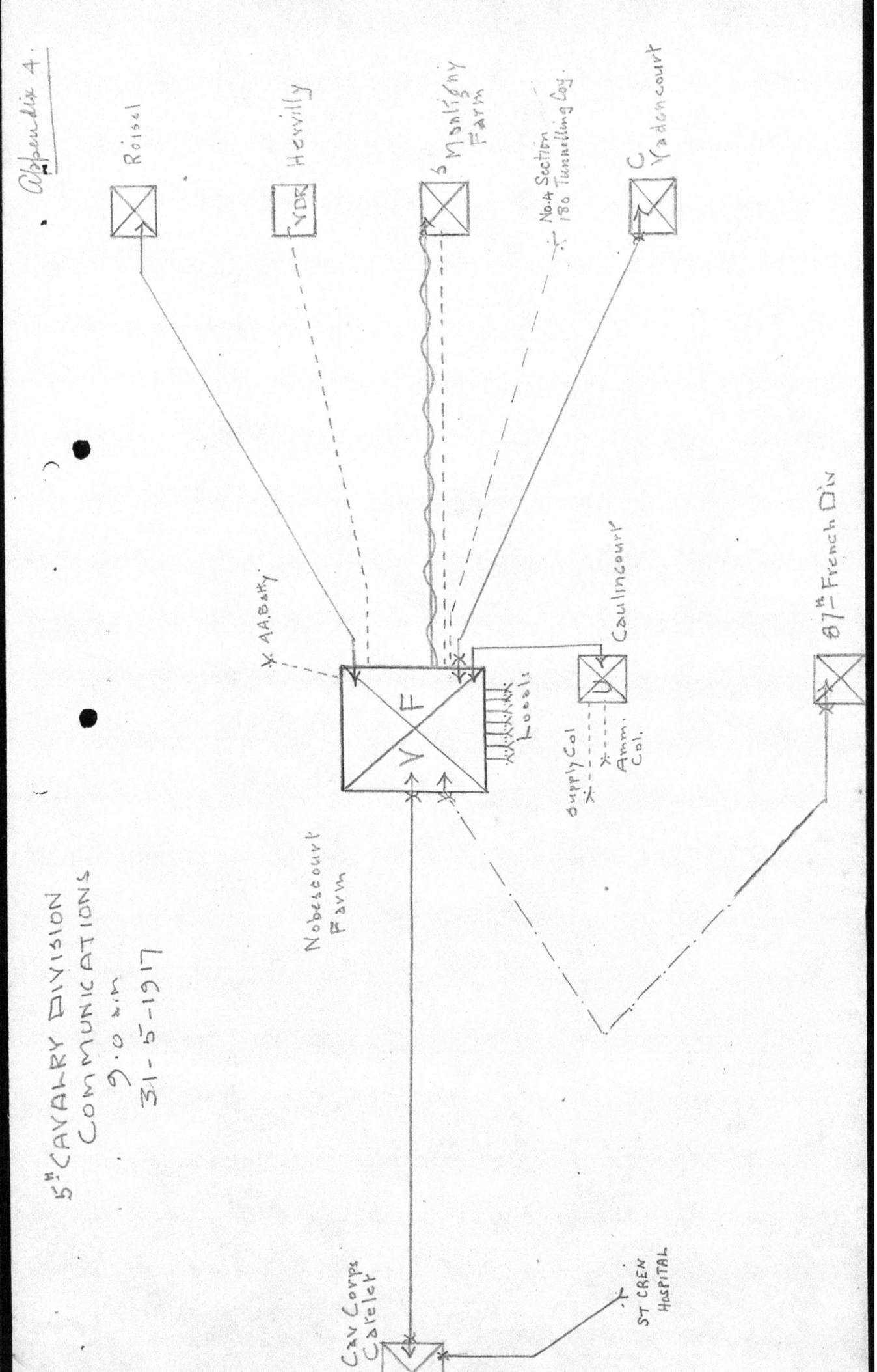

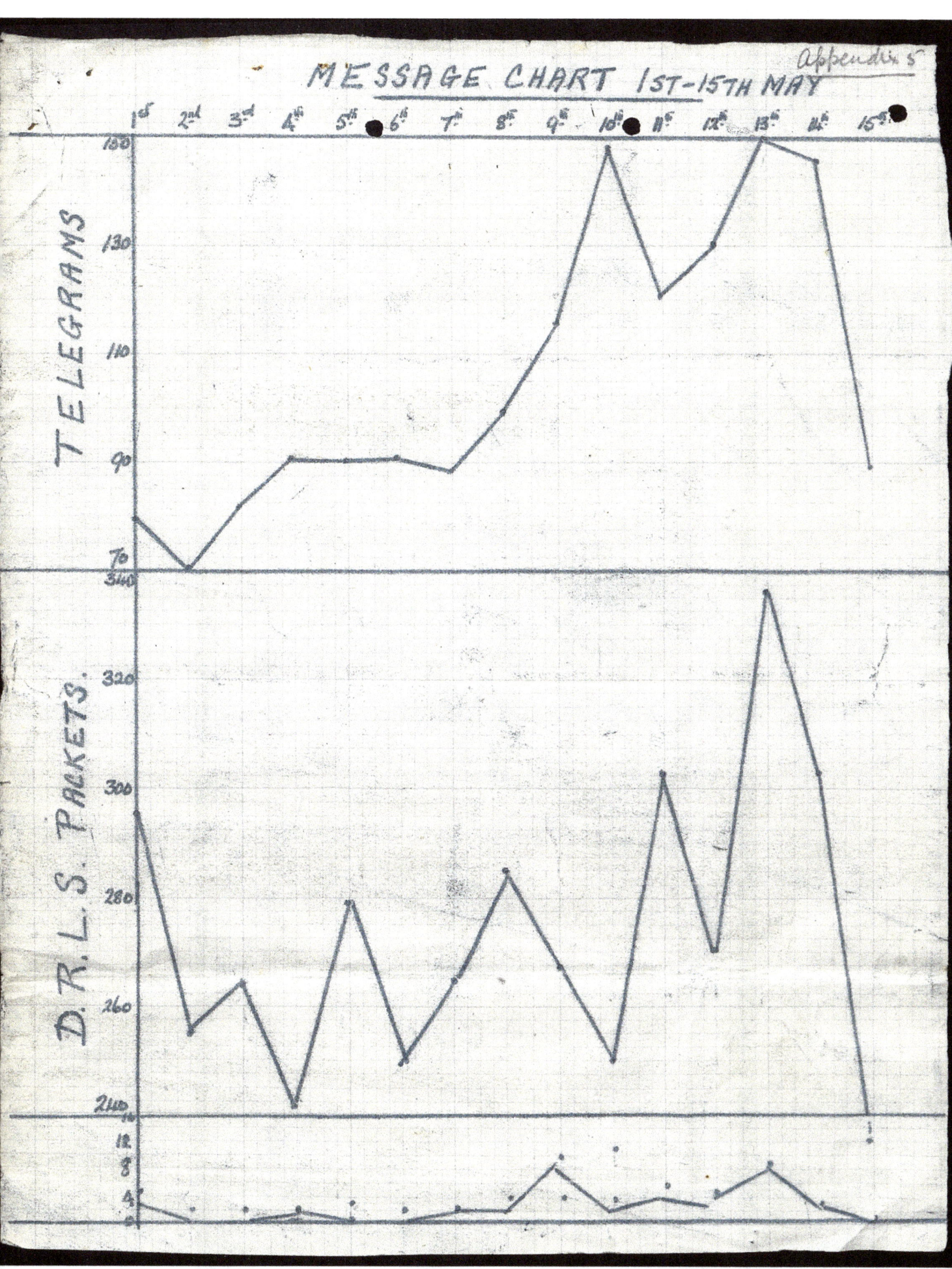

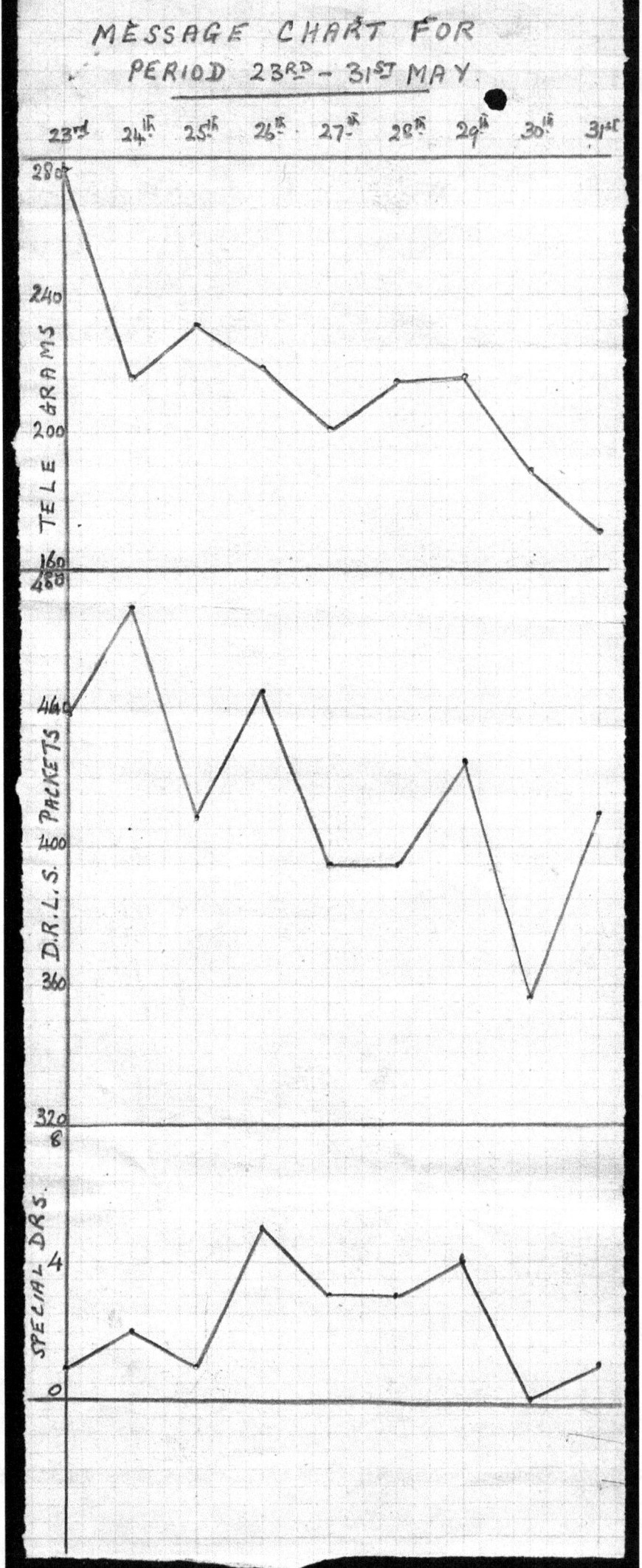

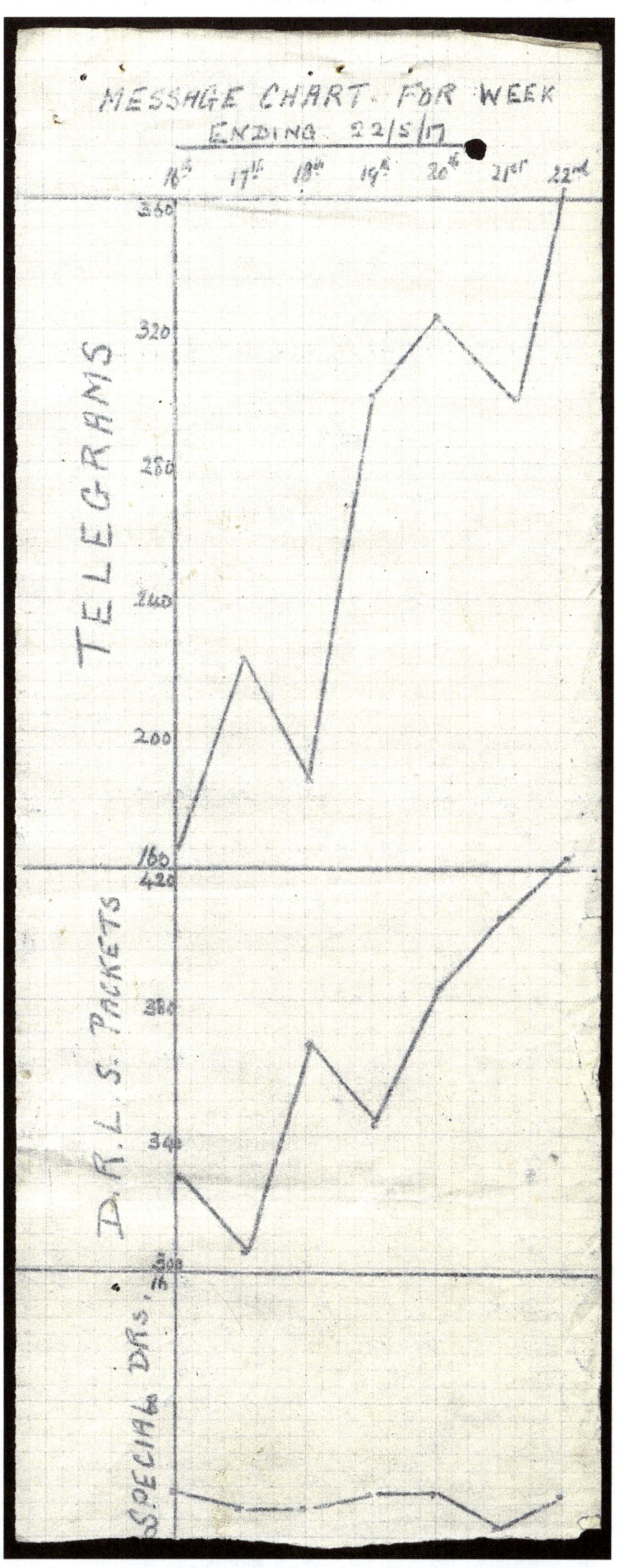

5th Signal Squadron
June 1917.

Army Form C. 2118.

WAR DIARY
or
INTELLIGENCE SUMMARY
(Erase heading not required.)

Instructions regarding War Diaries and Intelligence Summaries are contained in F.S. Regs., Part II. and the Staff Manual respectively. Title pages will be prepared in manuscript.

Hour, Date, Place	Summary of Events and Information	Remarks and references to Appendices
1/6/17 NOIRESCOURT FARM	Semi-permanent pair of airlines completed to Left Brigade (MONTIGNY FARM)	Ou.
2/6/17 "	Main Derving Station established at SUCRERIE N.W. of BARNES and connected by telephone at 3.50 p.m.	Ou.
3/6/17 "	Semi-permanent pair of airlines completed to VENDELLES by of 170 Tunnelling Coy. Semi-permanent pair of airlines completed by Corps Signals to BEAUVOIS to connection to French Division on right.	Ou.
4/6/17 "	Airline pair laid to Main Derving Station to replace cable.	
5/6/17 "	Airline pair laid to Anti-Aircraft Battery to replace cable. Permanent pair but through from CAVINCOURT to MORCHY LAGACHE for use of Canadian Brigade on arrival in back area. Relief of Rifle Brigade (Canadian) by Australian Bde. completed at 11.15 p.m.	Ou.
6/6/17 "	Communication by telephone with Canadian Bde. (MONCHY LAGACHE) at 9.25 a.m.	
8/6/17 "	11 p.m. Lines from SOMERVILLE WOOD and LONE TREE observed Posts in Right Bde. area - out by hostile barrage preliminary to a raid by Germans. Lines held as far forward as Wing Headquarters; communication to these from advanced Posts by runner.	Ou.

WAR DIARY or INTELLIGENCE SUMMARY

Army Form C. 2118.

(Erase heading not required.)

Hour, Date, Place	Summary of Events and Information	Remarks and references to Appendices
10/11 - 6-17 NOISESCOURT FARM	Thunderstorm during night caused damage to exchange at Right Brigade.	OUA
11-6-17 "	Two semi-permanent pairs completed between Left Brigade (MONTIGNY FARM) and JEANCOURT. One pair of airlines laid from JEANCOURT to Left Regiment of Left Brigade at L.28.a.5.5.	OUA
12.6.17 "	Two pairs of airlines laid from JEANCOURT to Reserve Regt. at Right Regt. at R.5.3.2. L.33.d.4.2, one pair extended on cable to dug-out.	OUA
12/13 6/17 "	During night raid was made on ASCENSION WOOD by party from Left Regt. of Left Brigade. Party entered wood at 2.10 and established communication with Left Regt. HdQrs by power buzzer at once.	OUA
13.6.17 "	One pair of airlines laid from JEANCOURT to Divisional Command Post at L.34.c.7.8. Naval scheme during night - communication obtained with both brigades. Line put through to TREFCON to back area.	OUA
14.6.17 "	Arrival in back area. During night relief of Left Brigade (Secundrabad) by Canadian Bde.	OUA
15.6.17 "	Telephonic communication obtained with Secundrabad Bde. in back area at TREFCON.	OUA

WAR DIARY
INTELLIGENCE SUMMARY

(Erase heading not required.)

Army Form C. 2118.

Hour, Date, Place	Summary of Events and Information	Remarks and references to Appendices
18-19-20/6/17 NOBESCOURT FARM	Owing to heavy thunderstorms on these days all circuits had to be disconnected at various times to prevent damage to instruments	OR
22/6/17 "	Pair of airlines between Right Artillery Brigade completed, also pair from Advanced Artillery Exchange (SMALL FOOT WOOD) to French Artillery Group on right.	OR
23/6/17 "	Pair of airlines laid from TERTRY to MONCHY LAGACHE (for use of Supply Column) & connected to permanent pair from TERTRY to CAULINCOURT. Line hut through to CAULINCOURT to use of Ambala Brigade on arrival in Back Area. Relief of Right Brigade (Ambala) H/4 Secunderabad Bde. took place during night. Communication obtained with Ambala Bde. at CAULINCOURT.	OR
24/6/17 "	Communications as per attached diagram.	OR
30/6/17 "	Message chart for month attached.	Appendix 1. " 2. OR

Alexander Capt.
O.C. 5th Signal Squadron

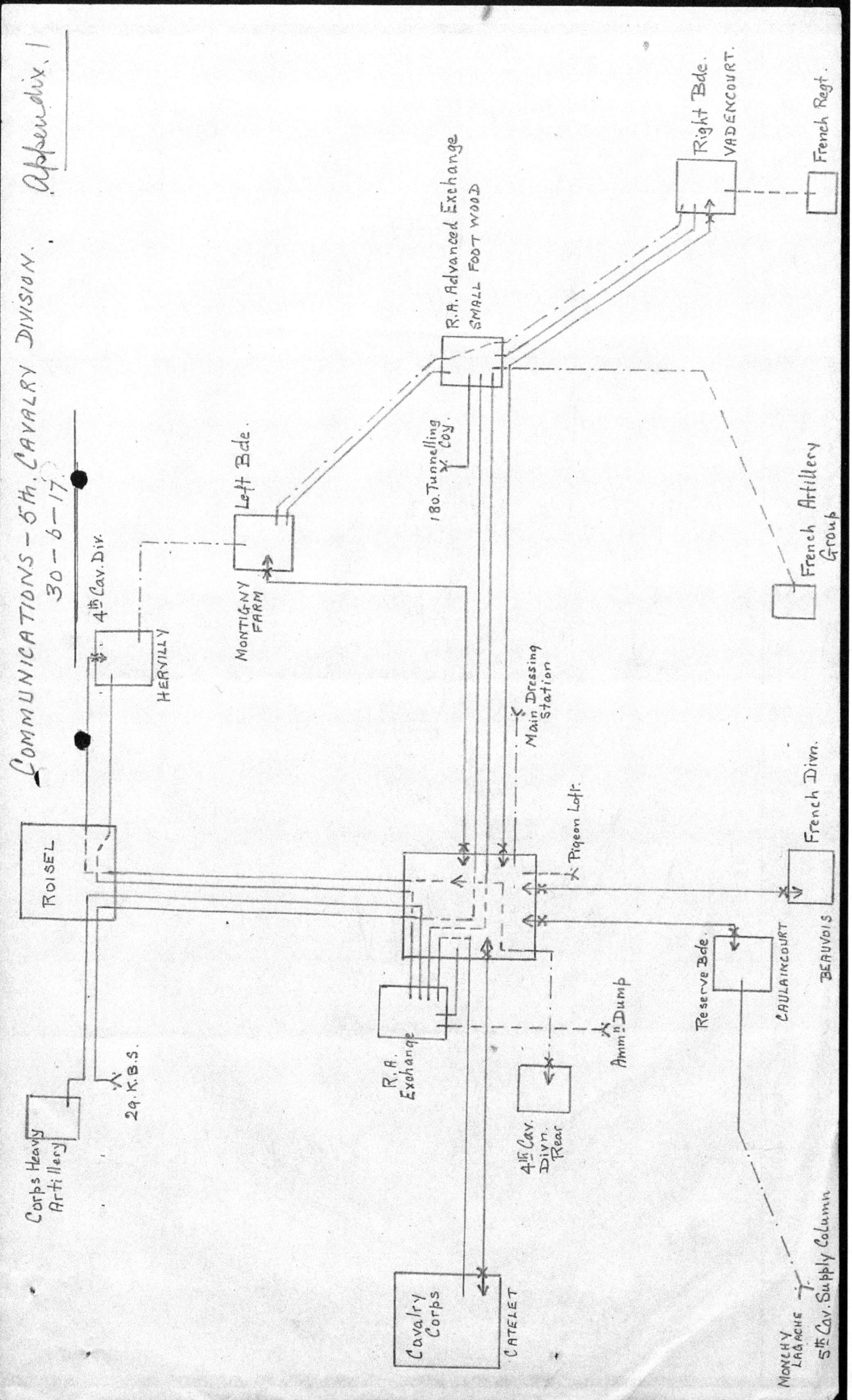

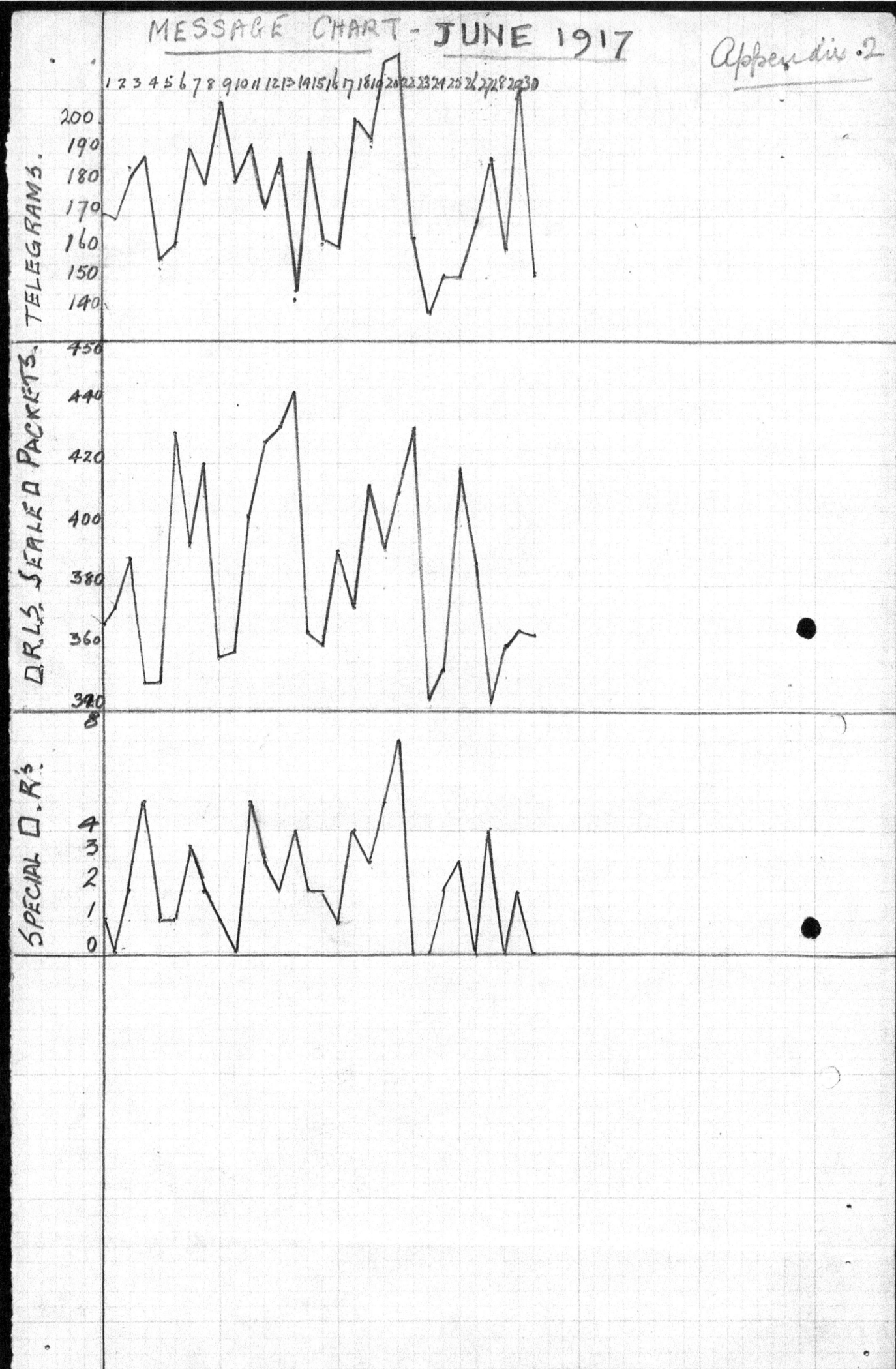

WAR DIARY — 5th Signal Squadron — Army Form C. 2118.

INTELLIGENCE SUMMARY

July 1917.

(Erase heading not required.)

Instructions regarding War Diaries and Intelligence Summaries are contained in F. S. Regs., Part II. and the Staff Manual respectively. Title pages will be prepared in manuscript.

Hour, Date, Place	Summary of Events and Information	Remarks and references to Appendices
1/7/17 NOBESCOURT FARM	Communications as at end of June 1917.	OR.
3/7/17 "	Two pairs airlines laid from point just West of VENDELLES to SMALLFOOT WOOD in order to give direct line from 29th Kite Balloon Section to Armoured R.A. Exchange, & also to connect 180th Tunnelling Coy. (VENDELLES) to R.A. Exchange	OR.
4/7/17 "	Pair of airlines laid to VRAIGNES to use of 101st Inf. Bde. (54th Divn.) on arrival.	OR.
12.45 pm 5/7/17 "	Telegraphic & telephonic communication obtained with 101st Inf. Bde.	OR.
5.30 pm 7/7/17 "	Australn. Cav. Bde. moved from CAULAINCOURT to CAUVIGNY FARM. Telegraphic & telephonic communication obtained to CAUVIGNY FARM at 6.30 pm.	OR.
8/7/17 "	Successful raid carried out during night by Canadian Cav. Bde. Cable run out with raiding party. Communication maintained until party started back.	OR.
2.30 pm 9/7/17 "	Line to Right Bde. (VADENCOURT) cut by shell fire; but through again during evening.	OR.
7.0 am 10/7/17 "	Armoured Report Centre left NOBESCOURT FARM and arrived BOUVINCOURT 7.45 am.	OR.
7.45 am " BOUVINCOURT	Telegraphic & telephonic communication obtained with Accumulated Bde. (TREFCON).	

Army Form C. 2118.

WAR DIARY
or
INTELLIGENCE SUMMARY
(Erase heading not required.)

2.

Instructions regarding War Diaries and Intelligence Summaries are contained in F. S. Regs., Part II. and the Staff Manual respectively. Title pages will be prepared in manuscript.

Hour, Date, Place	Summary of Events and Information	Remarks and references to Appendices
8.30 am 10/7/17 BOUVINCOURT	"G" + "Q" Staff connected to Exchange.	
9.0 am " NOBESCOURT FM	Signal Office handed over to Signals 58th Division on relief.	
9.0 am " BOUVINCOURT	Signal Office opened. Telegraphic Telephonic Communication obtained with Cavalry Corps.	
9.40 am " "	Telegraphic Telephonic Communication obtained with Ambulance Bde. (CAUVIGNY FARM)	
10.30 am " "	Telegraphic Telephonic Communication obtained with Canadian Bgd. (MORCHY LAGACHE).	
" "	Operation Order received from Division to march northwards between July 10th/11th	Appendix 1.
" "	Communications now as per attached diagram.	Appendix 2.
12 noon 13/6/17 BOUVINCOURT	Operation Order No.23 issued to march by Squadron to new area	
3 pm. 13/7/17 "	Ambulance Bde. marched to BUIRÉ. Communication maintained by DR.	
6 am 14/7/17 "	Canadian Bde. marched from MORCHY LAGACHE.	
6.30 am " "	Squadron mounted men transport left BOUVINCOURT to march with Canadian Bde.	
9.0 am " "	Squadron cyclist party left to form march with Canadian Bde.	
9.30 am " "	Ambulance Cav. Bde. arrived SUZANNE. Telegraphic Telephonic communication through Cavalry Corps.	
10.0 am " "	Canadian Cav Bde. arrived CAPPY. Telegrams circulated through Ambulance Bde.	
11.0 am " "	Squadron dismounted party arrived at ECLUSIER.	

Army Form C. 2118.

WAR DIARY
or
INTELLIGENCE SUMMARY

(Erase heading not required.)

Instructions regarding War Diaries and Intelligence Summaries are contained in F. S. Regs., Part II. and the Staff Manual respectively. Title pages will be prepared in manuscript.

3.

Hour, Date, Place		Summary of Events and Information	Remarks and references to Appendices
2 pm	14/7/17 BOUVINCOURT.	Secunderabad Bde. marched from TRÉFCON to BUIRE Communication maintained by DR.	
9.0 am	15/7/17 "	Advanced Report Centre left for TREUX. Secunderabad Bde. arrived at SUZANNE and took on line to Corps from Ambala Bde.	C.R.A.
11.0 am	" "	Advanced Report Centre opened at TREUX – intelegraphic and telephonic communication with Cavalry Corps thro' Secunderabad Bde. at SUZANNE.	
11.35 am	" "	Ambala Bde. arrived at TREUX. Canadian Bde. (HEILLY) in telephonic communication with Advanced Report Centre.	
12 noon	" "	III Corps took over from Cavalry Corps at CATELET.	
12.20 pm	" "	Direct telegraphic Communication obtained with Advanced Report Centre. III Corps being intermediate. Squadron mounted troops telephone at HEILLY.	C.R.A.
6.0 am	16/7/17 BOUVINCOURT	Main Report Centre closed. Left for ST POL. Report Centre in direct communication with III Corps.	
" "	" TREUX	Secunderabad Bde. arrived took over telephone communication to III Corps, telegraph being worked by Divisional Signals.	
10.20 am	" "	Main Report Centre opened.	
12 noon	" ST POL	Two telephone pairs put through to ST POL Exchange; 'G' Staff + G.S.O.1 connected to Division Exchange.	

1247 W 3299 200,000 (E) 8/14 J.B.C.&A. Forms/C. 2118/11.

Army Form C. 2118.

WAR DIARY
INTELLIGENCE SUMMARY
(Erase heading not required.)

Instructions regarding War Diaries and Intelligence Summaries are contained in F. S. Regs., Part II. and the Staff Manual respectively. Title pages will be prepared in manuscript.

Hour, Date, Place	Summary of Events and Information	Remarks and references to Appendices
16/7/17 ST POL	Communications with Brigades & Divisional Troops maintained by DR.	O/R
8 am 17/7/17 ST POL	Rear Report Centre closed at TREUX. "Q" Staff, O.C.A.S.C. & Signals Men connected to Exchange. Canadian Bde. Hdqrs. arrived at ST POL & connected to Exchange.	
3.30 pm " "	Ourdala Bde. at ROELLECOURT connected by telegraph & telephone. Communication with Secunderabad Bde. at ORVILLE maintained by DR.	O/R
3 pm 18/7/17 ST POL	Through to Cavalry Corps (AIRE) direct by telegraph & telephone.	
3.30 pm " "	Secunderabad Bde. at RAMECOURT connected by telegraph and telephone. Communication now as per diagram attached.	See Appendix 3
19/7/17 "	R.H.A. Bde. connected to Exchange.	O/R O/R
3 pm 20/7/17 "	Secunderabad Bde. moved from RAMECOURT to MONCHY CAYEUX. Communication maintained by DR.	O/R
3 pm 22/7/17 "	Canadian Bde. moved from ST POL to CROIX; telegraphic & telephonic communication obtained to new Hdqrs.	O/R
8 pm 25/7/17 "	Line completed to MONCHY CAYEUX and communication obtained with Secunderabad Bde. Communication now as per attached diagram.	O/R Appendix 4
30/7/17 "	Orders received for move of Divisional Headquarters from ST POL to HEUCHIN on 31 ST. Line put through from MONCHY CAYEUX to HEUCHIN.	O/R

1247 W 8299 200,000 (E) 8/14 J.B.C. & A. Forms/C. 2118/11.

Army Form C. 2118.

WAR DIARY
or
INTELLIGENCE SUMMARY.
(Erase heading not required.)

Instructions regarding War Diaries and Intelligence
Summaries are contained in F. S. Regs., Part II.
and the Staff Manual respectively. Title pages
will be prepared in manuscript.

Place	Date	Hour	Summary of Events and Information	Remarks and references to Appendices
ST POL	31st	9 am	Advanced Report Centre left for HEUCHIN.	
"	"	9.30 am	Squadron left for HEUCHIN.	
HEUCHIN	"	11 am	Communication obtained with Reinforcement Bde. (MONCHY CAYEUX) by telephone	
"	"	12 noon	Signal Office opened. Office also kept open at 17 Pol to communicate to Cavalry Corps + Ambala Bde.	
"	"	1 pm	'G' + 'A' Offices connected to Exchange	
"	"	1.30 pm	Communication obtained with Canadian Bde. at new hdqrs. (SAUTRECOURT)	A3.
"	"	4 pm	No.1 Mess + R.S.O. connected to Exchange. Communications as per diagram attached. Message chart for month attached.	Appendix 5 " 6

2/8/17

McDermont Capt.
Cmdg 5th Signal Squadron

Appendix. 1.

Communications - 5ᵀᴴ Cavalry Division
10-7-1917

Catelet

NCO

VF Bouvincourt

G.
G.S.O.1
Q
O.C.A.S.C.
A.H.A.
Signals

Amm. Col   PIC
Cauvigny Farm

PII Trefcon

Supply Column   PCA   Monchy Lagache

Appendix 2
Copy 3

5th Signal Squadron
Operation Order No. 23.

Reference Maps 1/100,000   13th July 1917

1. The Squadron will march to BRYAS between July 14th and 15th, grouped as follows:-

(a) <u>Main portion of Squadron</u>, under Lieut. JONES, will march with Divisional Headquarters under the orders of G.O.C. Canadian Cavalry Brigade. This party will parade to move off at 6.30 am outside the mounted mens billet.
The Cyclists, less those with Rear Report Centre, will accompany this party but will follow behind them parading outside the Signal office at 9 am under S/Cpl. Bray.
The 3 cyclists detailed to the Advanced Report Centre will halt at TREUX on the 2nd day's march.
The 2 N.C.Os with the cyclists are responsible for seeing that strict march discipline is maintained. S/Cpl. Bray will report daily to Lieut. JONES when all cyclists have arrived in camp.

(B) <u>Advanced Report Centre</u> (VFR) under Capt. ANDREWES will be composed as follows:-

Cpl. JAMES - N.C.O. i/c.
6 Motor Cyclist DRs.
Spr. Rattenbury (Motor Cycle)
" Liddell (Bicycle)
Pte. Scully "
Spr. Goodlet "

Cpl. Kirk will accompany Capt. ANDREWES in the Car, which will leave with the motor cyclists at 7am 15th
VFR will open at TREUX at 12 noon 15th July & will close at 8am 17th July.

(c) <u>Rear Report Centre (rF)</u> will be composed as follows:-

    Sergt. ATKINSON - N.C.O. i/c.
    7 Motor Cyclist DRs (incl. Cpl. Laws)
    3 Telegraphists (Spr. Jones & Ibbs, Pte. Roberts)
    1 Telephonist (Pte. Forrest).
    1 Instrument Repairer
    2 Pigeoneers
    Pte. Slinger rear.

Rear Report Centre will close at BOUVINCOURT at 12 noon 16th July and open at BRYAS at 8am 17th July.

Issued at 12 noon
Copy No. 1   Lt. Johns
  "   2   Sergt. Atkinson
  "   3   War Diary

R. Andrews
Capt
5th Signal Squadron

Appendix 3

Communications 5th Cavalry Division
18-7-1917

```
                                              ROLLECOURT
                                                  ◇
                                                  ×
                                                  P.G
                              ST.POL
                             Exchange
                                □
                                ×              ST.POL
    AIRE.                       └──◇
     □                             ×
 Z.co ◇──×─────────────────────×◇ VF ◇×────────×◇ P.11
                                ◇                 RAMESCOURT.
                                └─◇
                                  × 
                               ┌──┘
                            P.C.A ◇
                               □
                              ××××××××
                              │││││││
                              G G.S.O.1 O.C.A.S.C. R.H.A. Signals
```

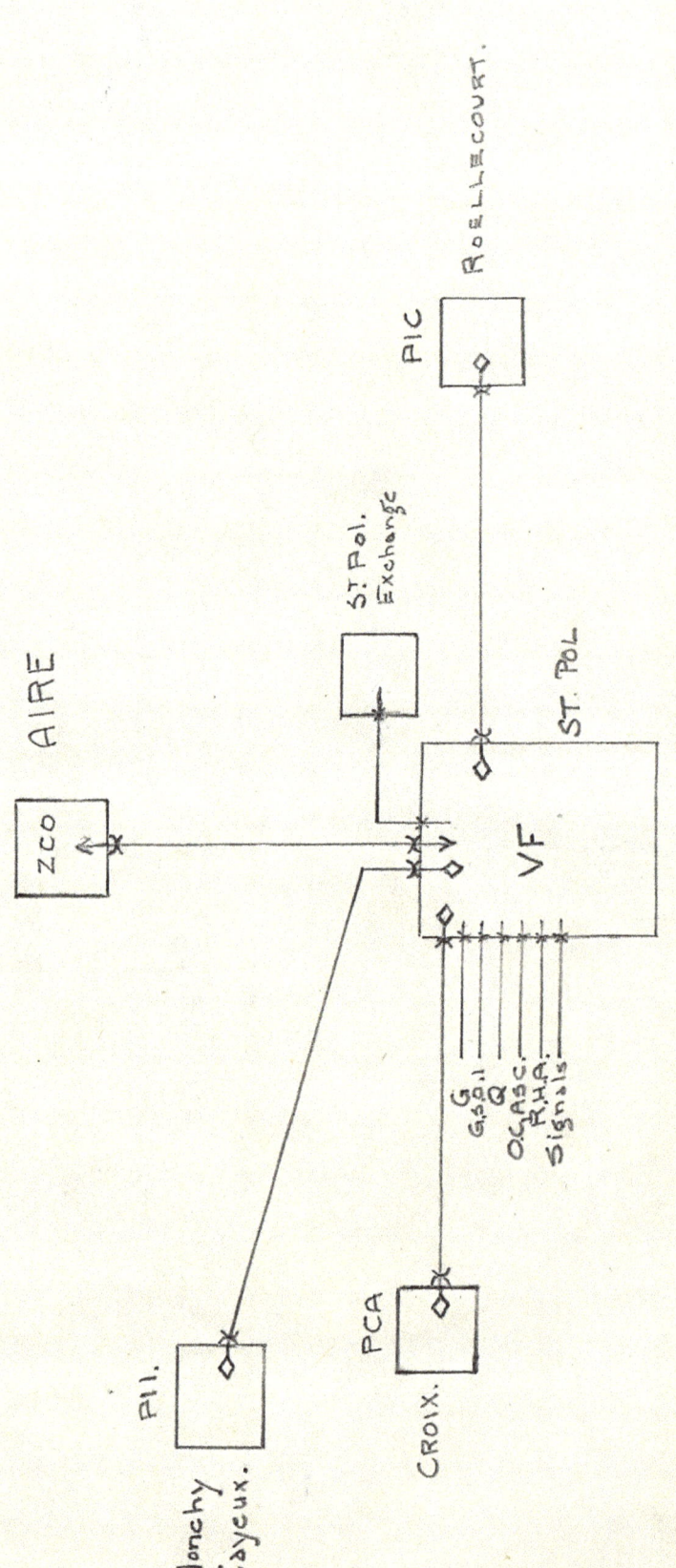

Appendix 5.

Communications 5th Cavalry Division
31-7-1917

HEUCHIN — YF
- G.
- Q.
- G.S.O.1
- No 1 Mess
- Signals

MONCHY CAYEUX — PII

SAUTRECOURT — PCA

ST. POL — VFR
— St. Pol Exchange

AIRE — ZCO

ROELLECOURT — PIC

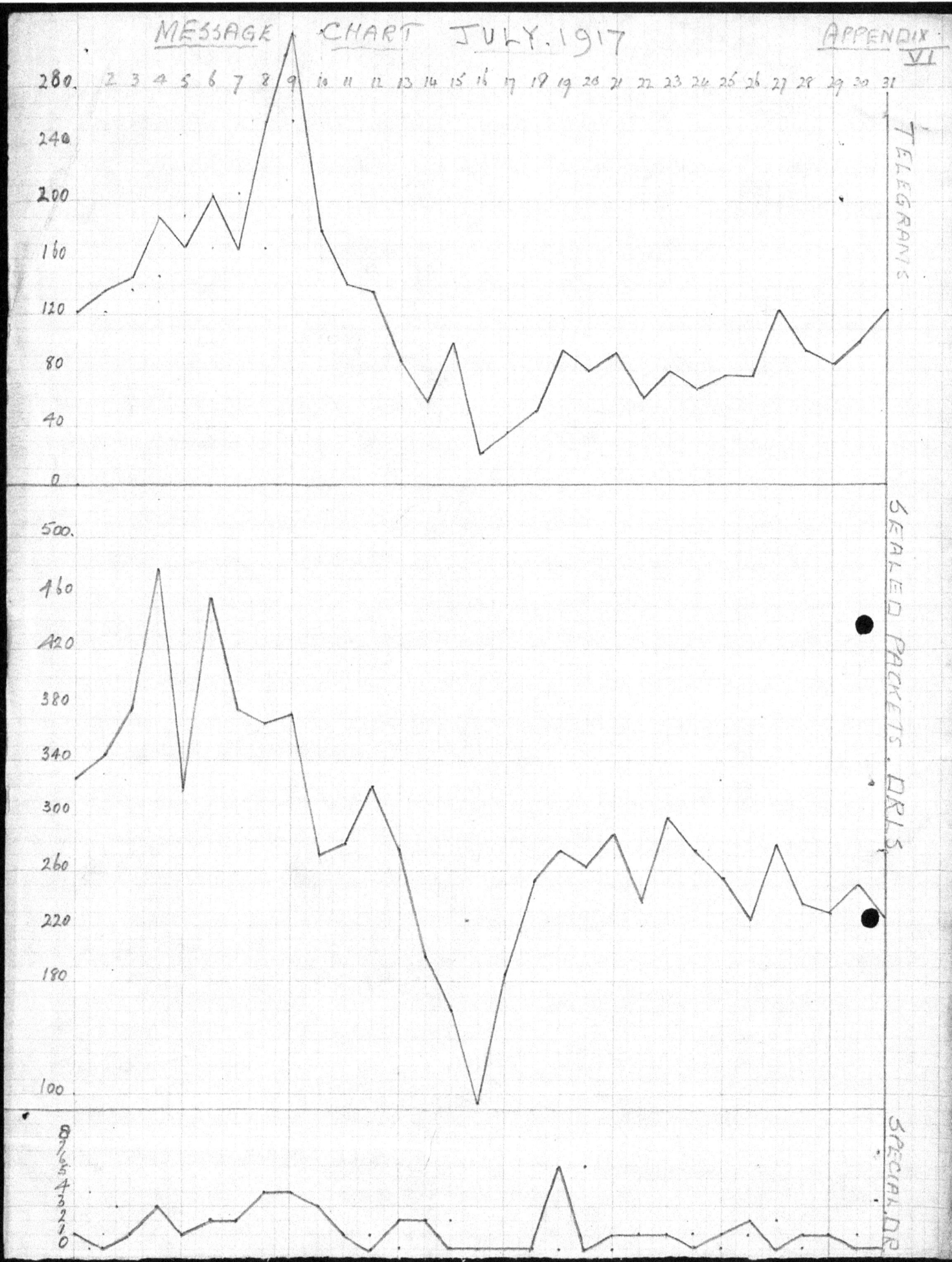

Army Form C. 2118.

WAR DIARY
or
INTELLIGENCE SUMMARY.
(Erase heading not required.)

5th Signal Squadron
August 1917

Instructions regarding War Diaries and Intelligence Summaries are contained in F. S. Regs., Part II. and the Staff Manual respectively. Title pages will be prepared in manuscript.

Place	Date	Hour	Summary of Events and Information	Remarks and references to Appendices
HEUCHIN	18/12/17		Squadron on line of march from recent school of Arts	
	14/8/17		New line put through to Cavalry Corps making line up France Bethune Sgn	
			HEUCHIN to PERNES Opened Arras Mai to Hesdine Rerouted via Pernes	
			HEUCHIN opened to Division 28 th Div 1ST D.C. Inf Bde etc	28/8/17 [App A]
			Opened I signal No News Commenced to use no 30 attached seizer.	
	30/8/17		Opened in various parts of Divn Various troops arrived	[Appendix]
			Rest of month uneventful	

W Repard Capt.
OC 5 Signal Squadron

HEADQUARTERS
No. 11
Date 1.9.17
5TH CAVALRY DIVN

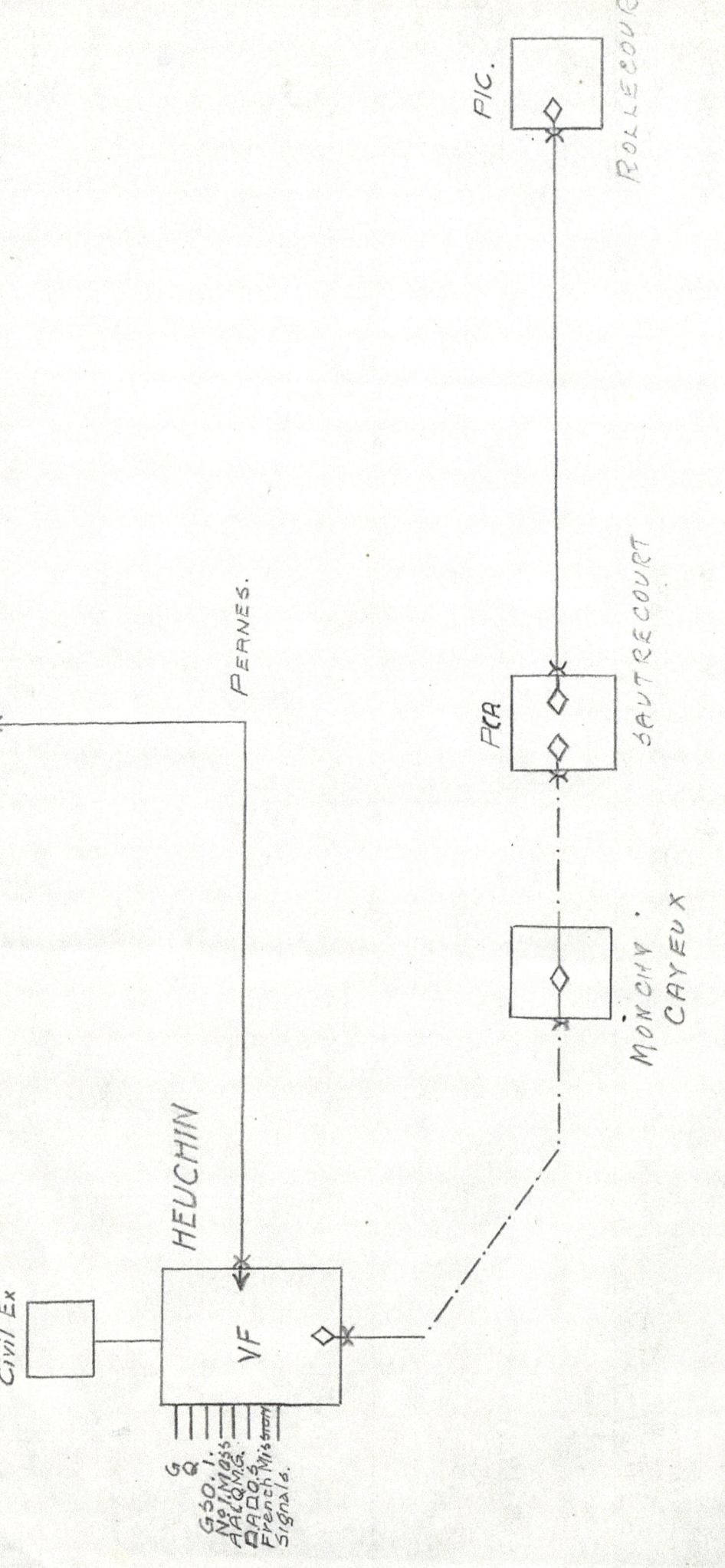

AUGUST 1917
TELEGRAMS, & D.R.L.S. PACKET CHART

Serial No: 149.

Army Form C. 2118.

5th Signal Squadron
September 1917

WAR DIARY
INTELLIGENCE SUMMARY.
(Erase heading not required.)

Instructions regarding War Diaries and Intelligence Summaries are contained in F. S. Regs., Part II. and the Staff Manual respectively. Title pages will be prepared in manuscript.

Place	Date	Hour	Summary of Events and Information	Remarks and references to Appendices
HEUCHIN	1/9/17	30/9/17	Squadron in same permanent billets. Communications as at end of August. Visual Training carried on. Record of messages attached.	
			5/10/17	
			H Raynal Capt.	
			Cmdg 5th Signal Squadron	

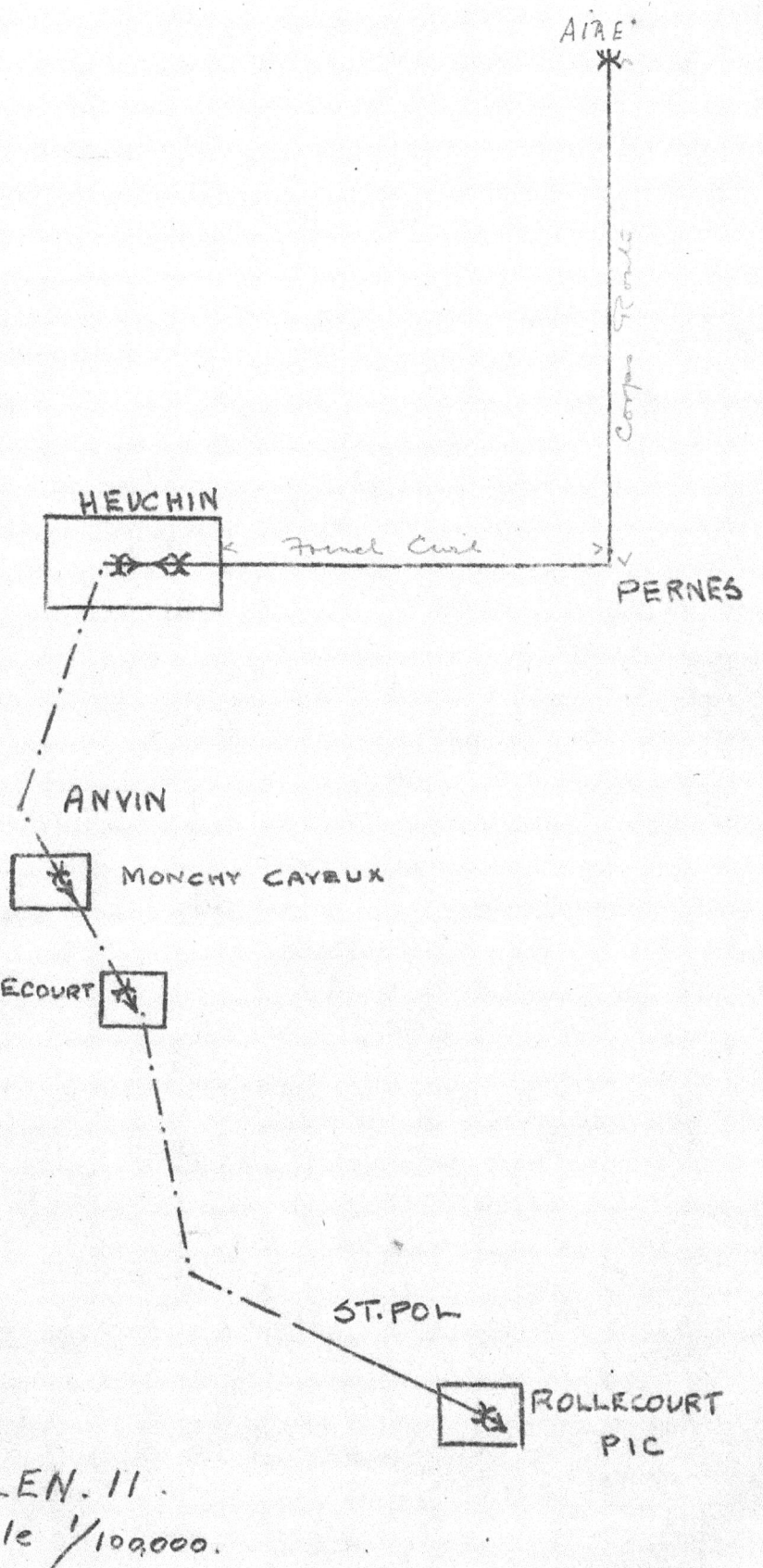

MAP. LEN. II.
Scale 1/100,000.

SEPTEMBER 1917
Telegram & D.R.L.S. Packet Chart.

WAR DIARY or INTELLIGENCE SUMMARY

Army Form C. 2118.

149

No 3 Signal Company .... October 1917

Place	Date	Hour	Summary of Events and Information	Remarks and references to Appendices
MEUCHIN	1/10/17 -5/10/17		Squadron in same permanent billets (communications as at end of September)	
	6/10/17	9.0am 10am	Advanced Report Centre left MEUCHIN for STEENBECQUE & arrived at 12 noon.	
STEENBECQUE	6/10/17		In communication with 3 C.B. by lines.	
		1.30pm	In communication with 3 C.O by horse & phone, and Car C.B by Phone	
	7/10/17	7.0 AM	Advanced Report Centre left to POPERINGHE and arrived at 8.20 AM (see Pt June Pub.)	
		9.45am	Advanced Office opened up. Rear report centre elsewhere	
		10.30am	Gen. Staff in direct communication with 18th Div Exchange by phone.	
		4.25pm	Adv. Report Centre in communication with 15th Div Exchange by phone	
			Telegrams distributed by Grapho 18th Div	
		5.30pm	In communication with POP Artillery Exchange. Telephone Ring via Y.R.	
		6.0pm	In communication with BII & TCA by phone via POP military Exchange	
		8.0pm 9.30am	In Comm. with PIC via Z.C.O by horse & phone. Pt James Pub, Cpl STEENBECQUE	
		6.0pm	In Comm. with PII by horse & phone.	
	9/10/17	10.30am	In Comm. with PCA by horse & phone.	
		5.30pm	In Comm with EAR closed by horse & phone. Comm with 18th Div ceased.	
	11/10/17	2.2pm	In Comm with PIC by horse & phone.	

WAR DIARY or INTELLIGENCE SUMMARY

Army Form C. 2118.

(Erase heading not required.)

Place	Date	Hour	Summary of Events and Information	Remarks and references to Appendices
POPERINGHE	14/10/17	8.30 AM	Ord. Report Battic left for RENESCURE	
		10 AM	Adv. Report Centre arrived RENESCURE	
		10.45 AM	In Comd (Colonel) to BAR by Motor	
		11.50 AM	1st (Canadian) Inf. Brigade came up to our Release	
		11.10 AM	Knitting house & platoon to TSAR	
		5.30 PM	In Com. with Pic Hd HARDRECQUES by Phone	
		11 MID	Rear Report Centre closed station at POPERINGHE	
			Own to ZCO via BAR & G.E.D by phone & wire	
			Own to P.99 & PCA by phone via TSAR & POP HQ	
RENESCURE	15/10/17	8 AM	Pic arrived station at HARDRECQUES & went to HERYARRE	
		8.30	P.99 Column arrived at KATOU & moved to HARDRECQUES	
		11.0	Adv. Report Centre left for FRESSIN	
		11.20	P.99 Opened up Comm at HARDRECQUES	
		3.0 PM	YE In Comm with PIC via TSAR & G.E.D by phone (at HERYARRE)	
FRESSIN	16/10/17	2 PM	PCA closed station (at Penera) and moved to MALHOVE	
		7.45 PM	P.99 Closed station at HARDRECQUES and moved to HERYARRE	

WAR DIARY or INTELLIGENCE SUMMARY

Army Form C. 2118.

Place	Date	Hour	Summary of Events and Information	Remarks and references to Appendices
FRESSIN	18/10/17	8:45am	Pte Good class at HERVARRE had head to MARESQUEL	
		11am	Rev. Robert Scott Church service at MAResQuel held	
			Practice Recruits march off.	
		1:45	Pte John Smart Coy on HERBURNE by Pferdes?	
		4pm	H.P. Junior class at HERBURNE by Majors ?	
			Foot Practice for Church	
			For Class ???? Bn ? Pte ????	
			??? ??? to ??? ????	
	19/10/17	11:25am	In Camp with Pte via HESDIN No HESDIN Gen S-Below	
			FRUSSECOLE	
	20/10/17		Pte A left HERVARRE for AIX-EN-ISSART Chapelles	
			Pere a Gen Lang & DR	
	21/10/17	2pm	Pte AC ????? via HESDIN + MONTREUIL by Plomont?	
	22/10/17	2pm	Through 16 PGA by ????	
	23/10/17	1pm	In direct com with P11 by hunt & Phone	
	24/10/17	4pm	In Con with Pte on new Div? pair to HESDIN	

WAR DIARY
or
INTELLIGENCE SUMMARY.
(Erase heading not required.)

Army Form C. 2118.

Place	Date	Hour	Summary of Events and Information	Remarks and references to Appendices
FRESSIN	25/10/17	9:35 AM	In Cmh with 2nd Dragoon Gds Regt by taking them to the Rif pain Pte Hare K gone up there bun to HESDIN + ben cover is by Pte alba though to MARESQUEL Barracks	
	1/11/17			

Ransom Cpt
OC 5th Signal Squadron

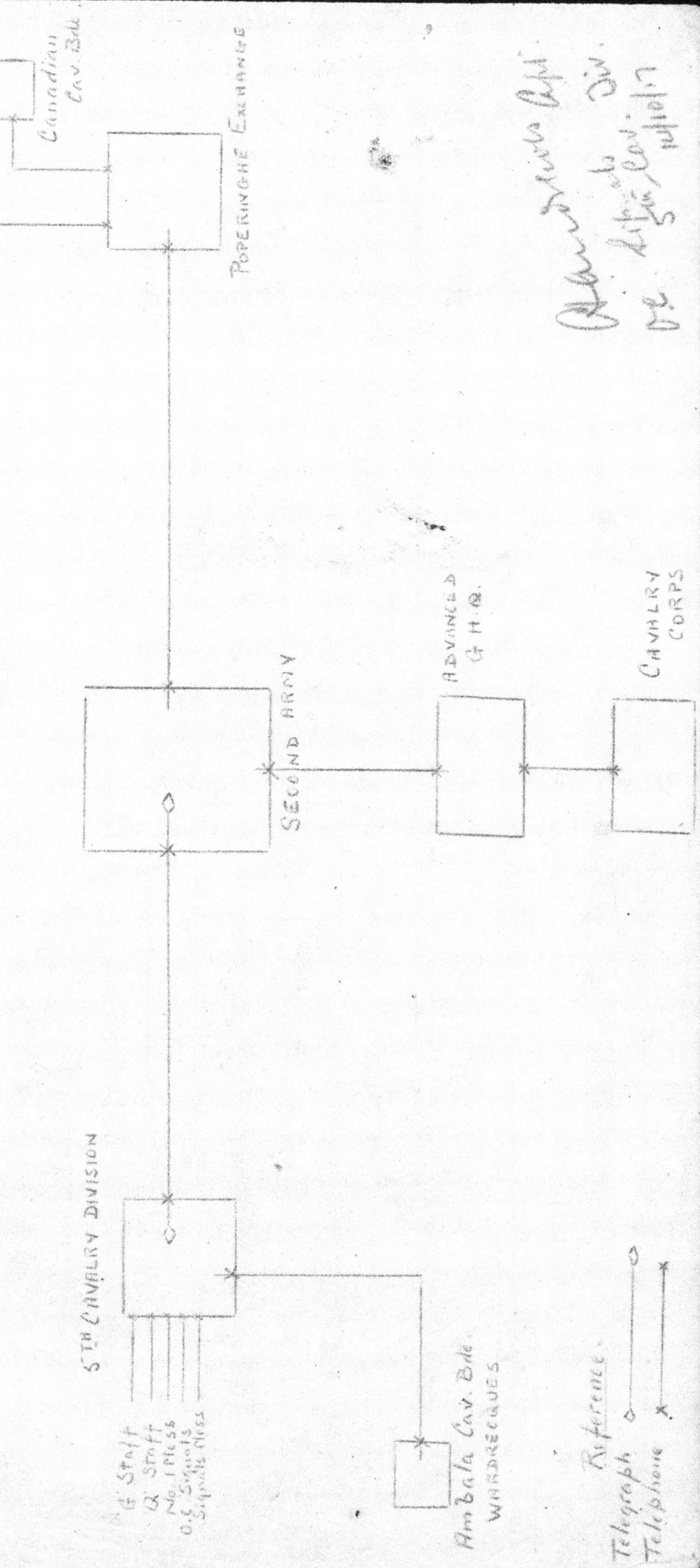

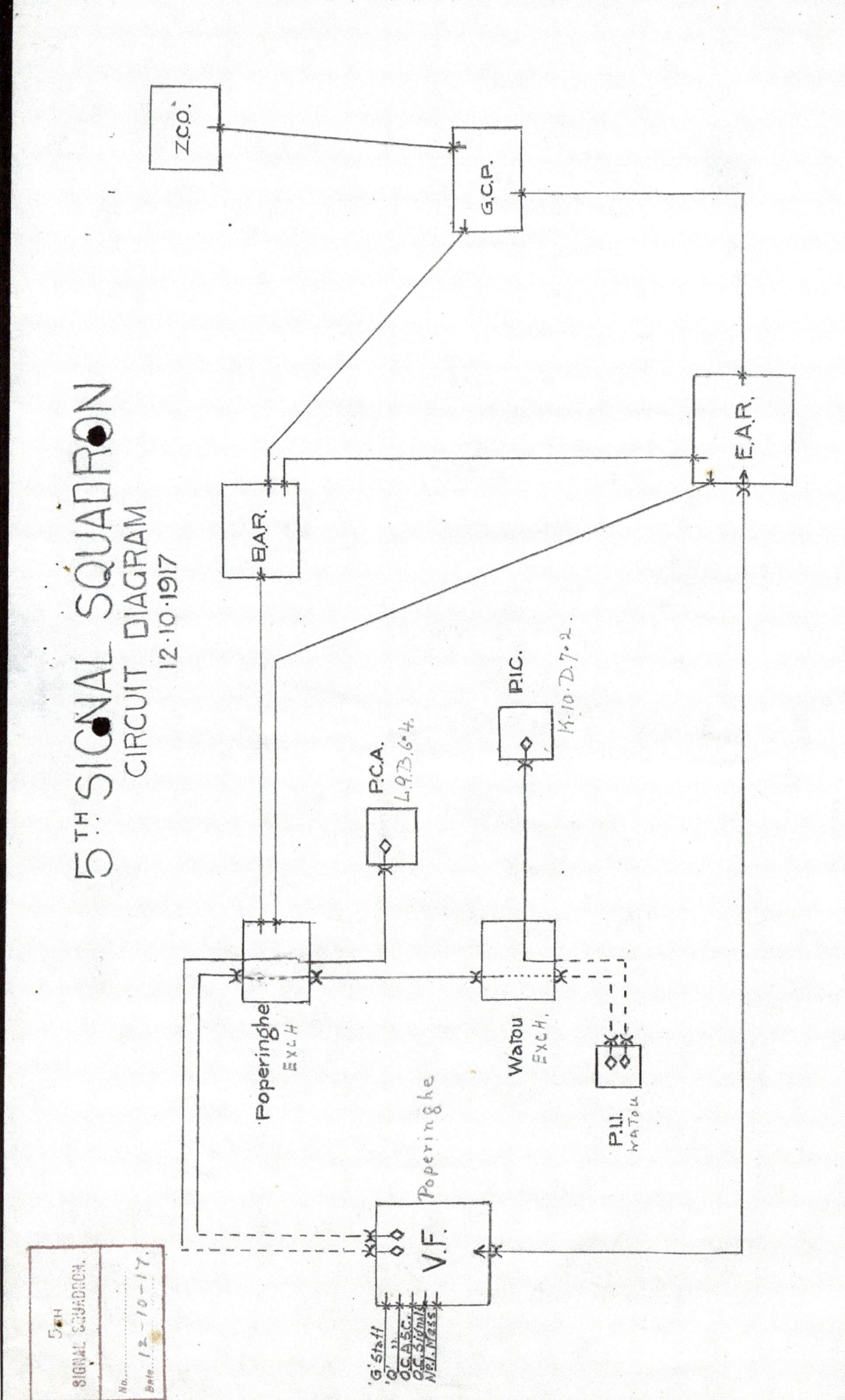

COMMUNICATIONS - 5TH CAVALRY DIVISION
NIGHT 15th/16th OCTOBER 1917.

- Canadian Cav. Bde.
- POPERINGHE EXCHANGE
- SECOND ARMY
- ADVANCED G.H.Q
- CAVALRY CORPS
- 5TH CAVALRY DIVISION
  - 'G'
  - 'A'
  - No.1 Mess
  - O.C. Signals
- Secunderabad Cav. Bde. WINDERGOUES
- Ambala Cav. Bde. HENVARRE

6.11.17

Diagram of
5th Cavalry Division
Communications

P/I Fruges

Ruisseauville
2nd Anzac Cav. Regt.

VF Fressin

'G' Staff
'Q' Staff
OC ASC
OC Signals
ADMS
OC Officers
DADOS
French Mission
Mol Mess
HQ Mess
Signal Mess

HD Hesdin

GCP

2CO

P/C Maresquel

PCA Aix-en-Issart

Montreuil

Operation Orders
by
Capt. C.L. Andrews, cmdg. 5th Signal Sqdn.

Reference map: 1/100,000 HAZEBROUCK

13/10/17

1. The Division is moving westwards tomorrow.

2. <u>Advanced Report Centre</u>, as per margin, will be ready to move off at 8.30 am, & will open up at RENESCURE at 11 am.
   <u>Lieut. Johns</u>
   Sgt. James
   6 Motor Cyclists
   Cpl. Kirk
   Spr. Odell
   Spr. Ibbs
   Box Car

3. <u>Mounted Men & Transport</u> will parade under Lt. Chase at 9.15 am.

4. <u>Bicyclists</u> under S/Sgt. Bray will parade outside the Signal Office at 8.30 am, & proceed direct to RENESCURE.

5. <u>Rear Report Centre</u>, as per margin, will close at 11am & proceed direct to RENESCURE.
   Cpl. Brinklow
   6 Motor Cyclists
   Spr. Rattenbury

Copy No. 1. A.S.M.
        2. Sgt. James
        3. War Diary

C.L. Andrews Capt.
O.C. 5th Signal Squadron

5th Signal Squadron. Operation Order No. 25

1. The march is being continued tomorrow to BONT DE LA VILLE.

2. The Mounted Men & Transport will parade at 10.15 a.m. & march under the orders of an officer to be detailed by the C.R.H.A.

   under Cpl. Bray
3. Bicyclists will parade outside the Signal Office at 10.0 a.m. & proceed to BONT DE LA VILLE via MANDREVILLES, THEROUNNE & DOHOM.

4. Report Centre, as for marching, will remain at .... (here) till further orders.
   Cpl. H.R.
   ...Northampton...
   ...
   ...Liddell
   ...Coleman
   ...David

Copy No. 1 to S.S.M.
   "   2 " C/pl Bray.
   "   3. War Diary ✓

Sanders
Capt
Cmdg. 5th Signal Squadron

78

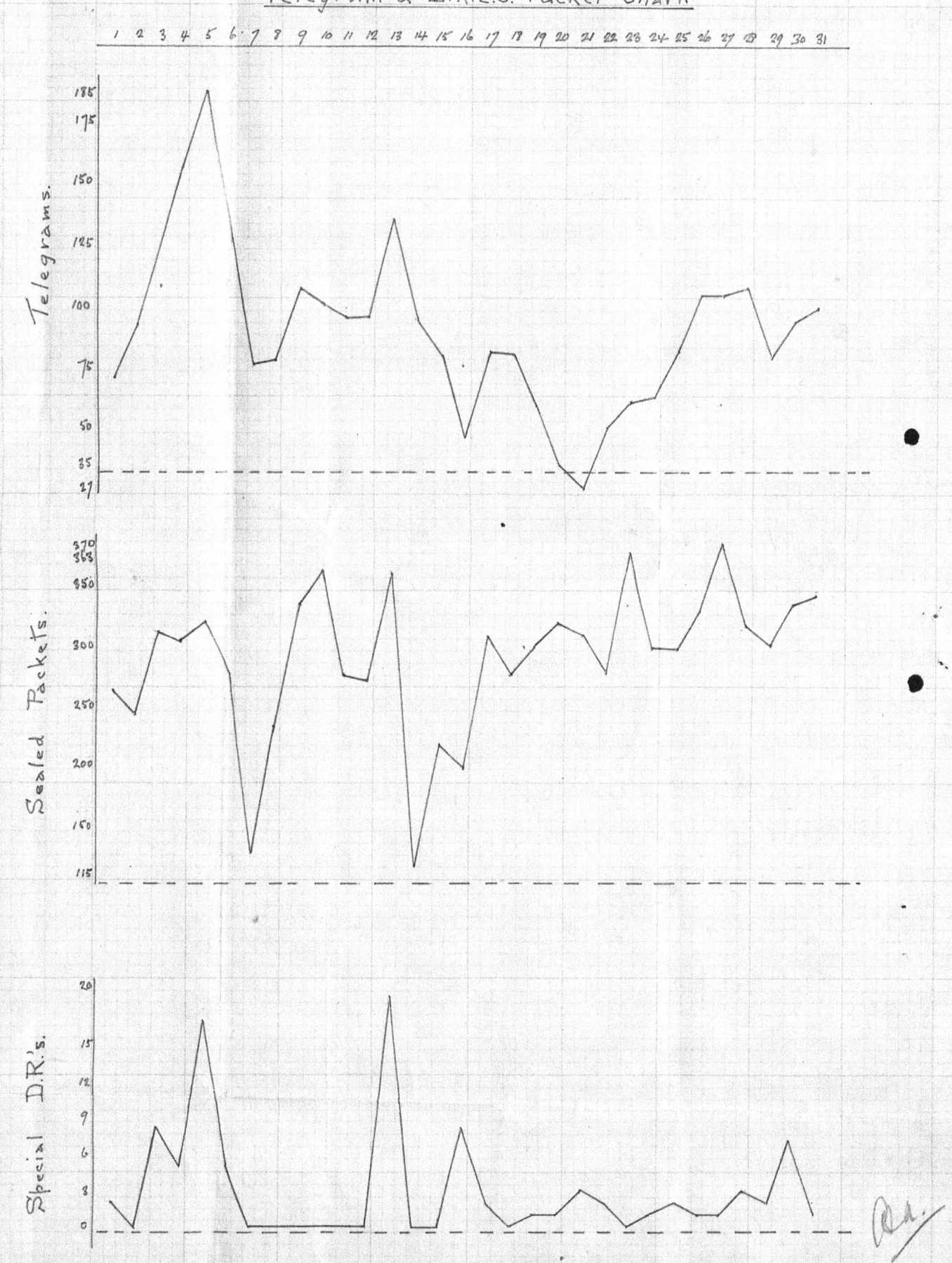

WAR DIARY or INTELLIGENCE SUMMARY

5th Visual Spotters
November 1917

Army Form C. 2118

Place	Date	Hour	Summary of Events and Information	Remarks and references to Appendices
BRESSY IN	7/11/17		Line to PCA at AIX-EN-ISSART is completed	
	9/11/17	3.30A	Advanced outpost section moves to MEZEROLLES	
	"	7.30A	P99 Report Centre opened at FROYES & Stns at the head of the platoon	
	"	8.30A	P9 C Closed down at MARESQUEL	
	"	9 AM	PCA Closed down	
	"	12.40A	Adv. R.C. VFR from the Ouen with Cavalry by a line through Doullens lights & BEAUVAL by motor Ihine to VF over aspect Control via GCR & HQ	
		12.55	Comn Established with PCA from MARESQUEL	
		1.30P	So Car built PIC at OCCOCHES which became an intermediate station between ZCD & advanced RC. PIC through to relay was as the Chin only	
			Comn with P99 by DR only. P99 hung up at MEILLARD	
	10/11	6.30A	PCA closed down at MARESQUEL	
		8.30	Col JAMES party moved to OCCOCHES	
		9 AM	Push expedient to HQ thru Egr to OCCOCHES	
		9.20A	Rota Opened RC Egt to Occoches from Rear Relay cents Egt Stns	
		9.40	Adv. R.C. in Cine by wires upper K ZCD	

Army Form C. 2118.

WAR DIARY
or
INTELLIGENCE SUMMARY.
(Erase heading not required.)

Instructions regarding War Diaries and Intelligence Summaries are contained in F. S. Regs., Part II. and the Staff Manual respectively. Title pages will be prepared in manuscript.

Place	Date	Hour	Summary of Events and Information	Remarks and references to Appendices
FRICOURT	10/11/16	11 AM	Recv R.C. rept fr. OCCOCHES Actg Report Centre on OCCOCHES left for BRAY	
OCCOCHES			Officer at OCCOCHES at same time being handed over to New Report Centre	
		2.15p	Adv. R.C. open up at CONTAY and in Comm with VP by Phone only	
		8.0p	Instructed by 3rd Army to attempt direct wire until next morning	
			P3D given to QUERRIEU & P1C to BEHEN COURT only comm possible	
			being D.R. P.C.A. moved to LE MEILLARD	
	11/11/16	Noon	Rear Report Centre moved to QUERRIEU	
		7.15A	Acto Report Centre at CONTAY in Comm with 2CO by Phone	
		9.45A	Advo R.C. at CONTAY in Comm with 2CO by wire & phone	
QUERRIEU		11.30A	Adv R.C. opens up at QUERRIEU Reping Officer at CONTAY open until noon	
		12.40p	In Comm with CAR by horse & Phone (delay caused by 3rd Army Pioneers)	
		4.32	Adv R.C. left QUERRIEU & moved to Lt SUZANNE	
		7.30	In Comm with CAR by horse & phone also to VF at QUERRIEU	
		8.30	In Comm with P1C at SUZANNE by Phone. P3D & Met. report by DR	
			PCA at FRAVILLERS, by DR	

Army Form C. 2118.

WAR DIARY
or
INTELLIGENCE SUMMARY.
(Erase heading not required.)

Instructions regarding War Diaries and Intelligence Summaries are contained in F. S. Regs., Part II. and the Staff Manual respectively. Title pages will be prepared in manuscript.

Place	Date	Hour	Summary of Events and Information	Remarks and references to Appendices
Bouvincourt	12/7/17	10:30A	Actv R.C. left SUZANNE for BOUVIN COURT. Officer at SUZANNE sent at 7am	
		3:10 p	Adv R.C. had a lin to VILLERS CARBONNEL	
		3:30p	In Com in with CAR by Phone	
		3:55p	In Com in with CAR by horse + Photo	
		5 pm	V/F.R. opened into arterial with V/F & CAR & later J. Columbia Q.	
		4:06 p.	PIC wired down & moved to CARTIGNY Cwn in by D.R.	
			PJD moved to VRAIGNES Cwn in by D.R.	
			PCA moved to SUZANNE & in phone at 8.25pm	
	13/7/17	1pm	In Cm in with PJD & VRAIGNES by Runners more in + photo	
		7pm	V/F.R. Closed down at SUZANNE	
	14/7/17	12:30p	In Com in with PIC at CARTIGNY by horse/photo on Car & Runner	
			PCA arrived at BOUCLY Cwn in by D.R.	
	15/7/17	10:55	In Cm in with PCA by Full relay horse photo	

WAR DIARY
or
INTELLIGENCE SUMMARY.
(Erase heading not required.)

Army Form C. 2118.

Place	Date	Hour	Summary of Events and Information	Remarks and references to Appendices
BOUVINCOURT	19/11/17	8 p.m.	Advanced about Guide moved to Z/W/S & established Office at 12·30 AM.	
	20/11/17	4 AM	Received report that in Com. with ZRC by wire & Phone.	
		12·30 AM	Recd Report Centre closed station at BOUVINCOURT	
Z/W/S		12 Noon	The Signal Signature (Lieut J---) moved to R9B8.8 (W/W/W/5.97C) +	
R9B8.8 (W/W/W 57C)		4 p.m.	Established Office. In Com with ZRC in Camp only 6 p.m. by DR	
			In Com with PC by Lamp & DR	
		6·0 p.m.	They have left behind at Z/W/S to keep a small rear party (Lieut Healy) In Com in with XS by H.Lamp. Rear Party by wt to XS (Capt Healy)	
		1100 yds N.E. of VILLERS-(FAUCH) 21·37 In Com with 15 PA by Lamp. In Com with 15 PA by DR.			
EQUANCOURT	22nd		Report Batt'n returned to EQUANCOURT leaving a small party at R9B8.8 with +	
		11·30	Taken VF batt established + rear party (Capt--)	
		12·30 p.m.	VF in Com with ZRC by horse & Phone. In Com with Rear by DR	
SUZANNE	23rd	8·30 AM	VFR moved to SUZANNE	
		12 Noon	In Com in with ZOO by Phone & ZRC by horse + Phone & DR	
		MON	Rear Report Centre closed at EQUANCOURT	
		7·10 p.m.	In Com with Rear Btn by Phone	

Army Form C. 2118.

WAR DIARY
or
INTELLIGENCE SUMMARY.
(Erase heading not required.)

Place	Date	Hour	Summary of Events and Information	Remarks and references to Appendices
SUZANNE	23/6/17	10.30p	In Cmn with Pie by Phone & by lettre early next morning	
	24/6/17	12.30p	In Cmn with P.11 by Phone thro' Pie exchange	
	27/6/17	7.30 AM	A.O. Rep Cullen left for Morchy-Lagache	
		10.A.M	In Cmn with ZCO by phone	
Morchy-Lagache	12 noon	Rear Rep Cullen left Suzanne		
	12.35pm	In Cmn with ZCO by Horse & Plane		
	12.30pm	In Cmn with PLA by plane & on wilk relieve D3 Kessel		
	4 pm	In Cmn with Pie by plane		
	28th	9.40 AM	In Cmn with P99 thro' Pie Exchange	
		2.30 PM	In Cmn with full Sqdn by plane	
		3 hour	4 Mid van when ennwhere to Teriny.	
	29th	11 AM	Rew Rep of Cullen left for Villers-Faucon	
	30th	12.45 PM	Moved in at Villers-Faucon in preparate with 55th Div Signals	
		1.30 pm	Used stren at 55th Div Hrs to (ESA) ref map 62 C	
		3 pm	Opened up at (ESA)	
		8.20 pm	In Cmn with ZRC by Phone & horse by Runners at 8.35pm	

Army Form C. 2118.

WAR DIARY
or
INTELLIGENCE SUMMARY.
(Erase heading not required.)

Place	Date	Hour	Summary of Events and Information	Remarks and references to Appendices
At G2C. 6.15.A	30/4/17	5.30pm	Lnm with PCA by visual & with LR DR? PCor (H17c7.4)/Ha (W16D5.2)	
		6.15pm	Lm lnm with PCA by visual LR DR? PCA or (X19A2.3) P22 in GOUZEAUCOURT writing in lmm by miraled DR?	

Lieutenant Col.
Be Salcher Regutur

5TH SIGNAL SQUADRON
Diagram of Communications

9/11/17

FRESSIN
VF

HD
PCA

G.C.P.

DOULLENS

PIC
OCCOCHES

VFR
MEZEROLLES

Z.C.O.
BEAUVAL

W. R. Jobbs Lieut

10.11.17

5TH SIGNAL SQUADRON
DIAGRAM OF COMMUNICATIONS

CAR

VFR

DOULLENS

X
ZCO
BEAUVAL.

OCCOCHES
VF

A.B. Jekes Lieut

11.III.17.

5TH SIGNAL SQUADRON
DIAGRAM OF COMMUNICATIONS.

A.D. John Ruck

ZCO
[BEAUVAL]

ALBERT
[CARY]

VE
[QUERRIEU]

SUZANNE
VER
PIC.

5TH SIGNAL SQUADRON   12:11:17

DIAGRAM OF COMMUNICATIONS

VF — Bouvincourt

PCA — Suzanne

CAR — ALBERT

ZCO — BEAUVAL

A.D. Johns Lieut.

13/11/17

Circuit Diagram of
5th Cav. Div. Communications

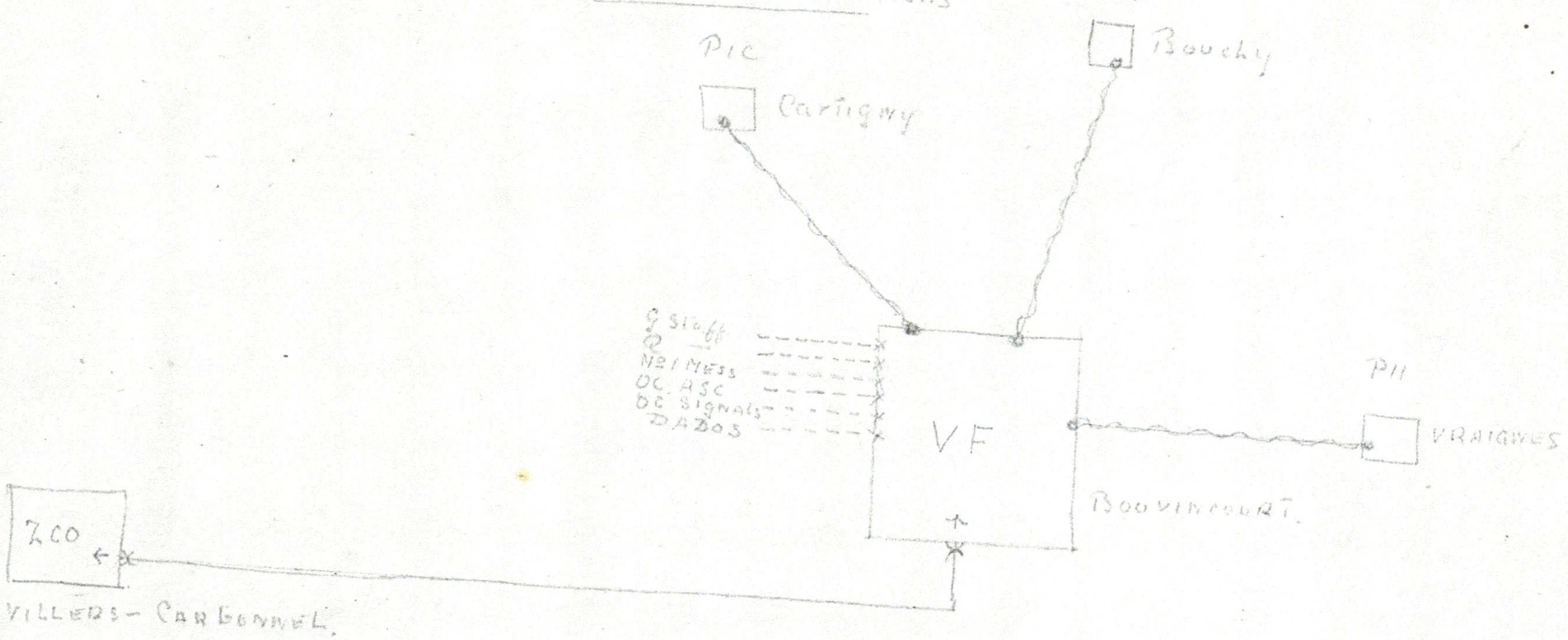

PCH Bouchy
PIC Cartigny
VF
Boovincourt
PII Vraignes

Staff
No 1 Mess
OC ASC
OC Signals
DADOS

ZCO
Villers–Carbonnel

(13) 3 hrs news

26/11/17

Circuit Diagram of
5th Cav. Div. Communications

[2RC]   5ins

G. Staff ---- [VF] E. Edge of Fins

A.B. Johnston

20/11/17

DIAGRAM OF COMMUNICATIONS
5th CAVALRY DIVISION.

O.B. Johns Sqn

22/11/12

O.B. John Laur?

Diagram of Communications
5th Cavalry Division

```
                              [ ZAC ]
                               ↑ 7ins
                                |
                                |
                                |
                                |
                                |
                                |
                                |
  Equarycourt                   |
  [ ↙ ]-------------------------
  ≡≡≡
  Q Staff
  A Staff
  OC Signals
```

24:11:17

CIRCUIT DIAGRAM
of
5th Cav Div Communications

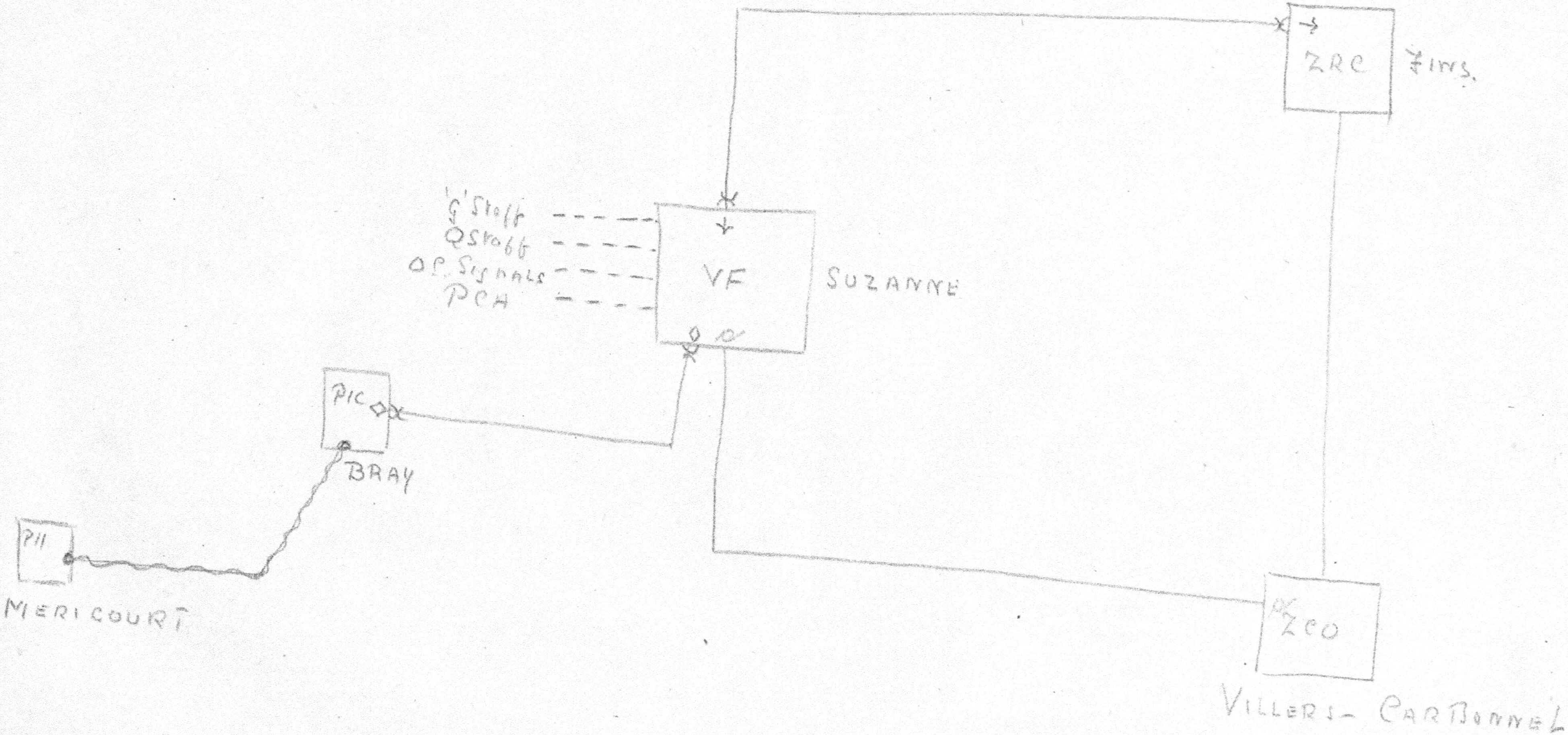

[ZRC] ‡ ims.

[ZEO] Villers-Carbonnel

[VF Suzanne]
G Staff
Q Staff
OC Signals
PCH

[PIC] Bray

[P11] Mericourt

AJ Johns

23rd Nov 1917.

5th Cavalry Division
Circuit Diagram.

- PCA — Mereaucourt.
- PIC — Tertry
- PII — Trefcon.
- D — Field Sqdn.
- VF — Monchy-Lagache
  - 'G' Staff
  - 'Q' Staff
  - HQ Mess
  - O.C Signals
  - AA+QMG
  - OC ASC
  - DADOS
  - Fr. Mission
- Caulaincourt
- Z.C.O

O.R. McPuer

WAR DIARY or INTELLIGENCE SUMMARY

Army Form C. 2118.

DECEMBER 1917

7th Dragoon [?]

(149)

Place	Date	Hour	Summary of Events and Information	Remarks and references to Appendices
ESASO	3/12		In Camp with Cavalry Corps Adv at VILLERS-FAUCON by telegraph	
Map 57.C 1/20000			Relieved & withdrew. In Bn. W.L.C. Cavellero Relieved at K.24.B.2.2 arrived at	
			Ambala Bde at hd 16 DSO by Camp Mid Dr. See Bn & Bde Nn. 9/1002 &	
			Jodpur Bde 17th moved G K.29.A.2.7 right half the at arriving Bde SAH by	
	11 AM		6th Jodpur Cav. sett Ambala Bde at Stable Catherine	
	12.30pm		Ambala Bde moved to REVELON FARM and Bn. Nth Westminster Dragoons	
			Koolin [?] [?] from K16 D8.0 to REVELON Fm	
	1.30pm		The Sect'ed Bde camped in the Ambala Bde area by K. Upton Fm	
	2.50 am		Move to Telephone comms with Cavalry Bde at K.14.D.2.2 Bn & Sqdn Hdqrs Bn	
			Jodpur Bde later own from their Ambala Bde at Revelon Fm and	
			allotted 1st Posn from them to K29.A.2.8	
			Ambala Bde arrived at K.29.A.2.8	
2/12/17	2pm		Bn. Advd party movd to HEUDICOURT and at 1st Saxons Engrs to Cable	
			also went entrances the line from ESASO (Rd hds 620) to HEU DICOURT	
	5.31pm		Bn R.G. stood down at ESASO	
			A Bde Gen. St intended from Bde Hd to HEUDICOURT	

Army Form C. 2118.

WAR DIARY
or
INTELLIGENCE SUMMARY.
(Erase heading not required.)

Instructions regarding War Diaries and Intelligence Summaries are contained in F. S. Regs., Part II. and the Staff Manual respectively. Title pages will be prepared in manuscript.

Place	Date	Hour	Summary of Events and Information	Remarks and references to Appendices
HEUDICOURT	2/2/17	6pm	We had a few of orders to 1st Res Bde at M.19.95.6	M.19.95.6
	3/2/17	11am	Our Adv. Party started to LONGAVESNES	
		12noon	Res Party started for LONGAVESNES	
LONGAVESNES		1pm	We lay down & left for our Sig Office to 1st Res Bde & same to LONGAVESNES	
			With the 2nd Bde we came with Bde Capt Bde & 1st Res Bde On Bde Pos	
			All our Wagons we housed with 1st Res Bde Sig Office	Returned S.2.C
			Ambulance Bdes moved to E.29.A.d.8 Res Gas Bde 6th FIELD A – M.40.B.D.	
			Red Cross Bde went to K.16.6.65 (Horse) Our Communications	
			& line trans only by D.R. at ho that will	
	4/2/17	12.30pm	We laid a single Cable line to Satur Bde & been telephoning to Do	
	6/2/17	2.30pm	We laid a single Cable line to R.H. Balrn telephones from Do	
	9/2/17	11am	Our fore party moved to MONCHY-LAGACHE & took over the Sigs	
			With them the party of 2pdr Wheels three Bn the Regt	
		2pm	Our party Bde moved down at LONGAVESNES and moved the Res Bde Sig to MT of Bde Orders (which has taken along the line to 1st Cav Divisn	

Army Form C. 2118.

WAR DIARY
or
INTELLIGENCE SUMMARY.
(Erase heading not required.)

Place	Date	Hour	Summary of Events and Information	Remarks and references to Appendices
Mouchy-LaGache	8/12/17		Aubala Bde moved to CARTIGNY. Sec/Bdr Bde moved to V.4.C.7.4. Can Bde in reserve at ROISEL, only available Bde in DR.	7/8/62 C
	9/12/17	6:30pm	In telephonic and telegraphic Comn with Can Bde and Can Corps and 24th Division	
	10/12/17	1:30pm	In telephonic & telegraphic comn with Sechas Can Bde by a Shy A Calba Pau.	
	15/12/17	1:45pm	In telephonic Comn with 5th Field Squadron at (W.87.3.2.8)	no 62 C
	16/12/17	10:30am	Sec/Bd Bde closed down at V.4.C.7.4 and moved to TREFCON	
		12:40pm	In telephonic and telegraphic Comn with its Sec/Bd Bde on permanent Run	
		3:45pm	Can Bde left ROISEL and moved to MEREAUCOURT	
		4pm	Home telephonic Communication with Can Bde	
		6pm	In telephonic & telegraphic comn with Can Bde	
	23/12/17	12:35p	In telephonic Comn with Aubala Bde on permanent lines	
		1:40pm	In telephonic Comn with 2d Div. Ordinance Dump at Q.30.C.26	7/62 C
		3:45pm	In telegraphic + telephonic Comn with Aubala Bde at TERTRY.	

A. Andrzjowski Lieut.
Ft. S. Signal

1st Dec 1917

5TH SIGNAL SQUADRON
CIRCUIT DIAGRAM

Ref. Maps Sheets 57c & 62c
1/40,000

A: I

Revelon Farm

[P11]

[PIC] (W29 A 2.3)

[PEA] (W24 B 2.2)

b'Staff...... (E 5 A 5.0)

[VE]
W.

W.

[ZRC]
Villers-Faucon

A.B. Lines. Sig. E
A.B. Lines. Sig. E
c/o John Sig. E

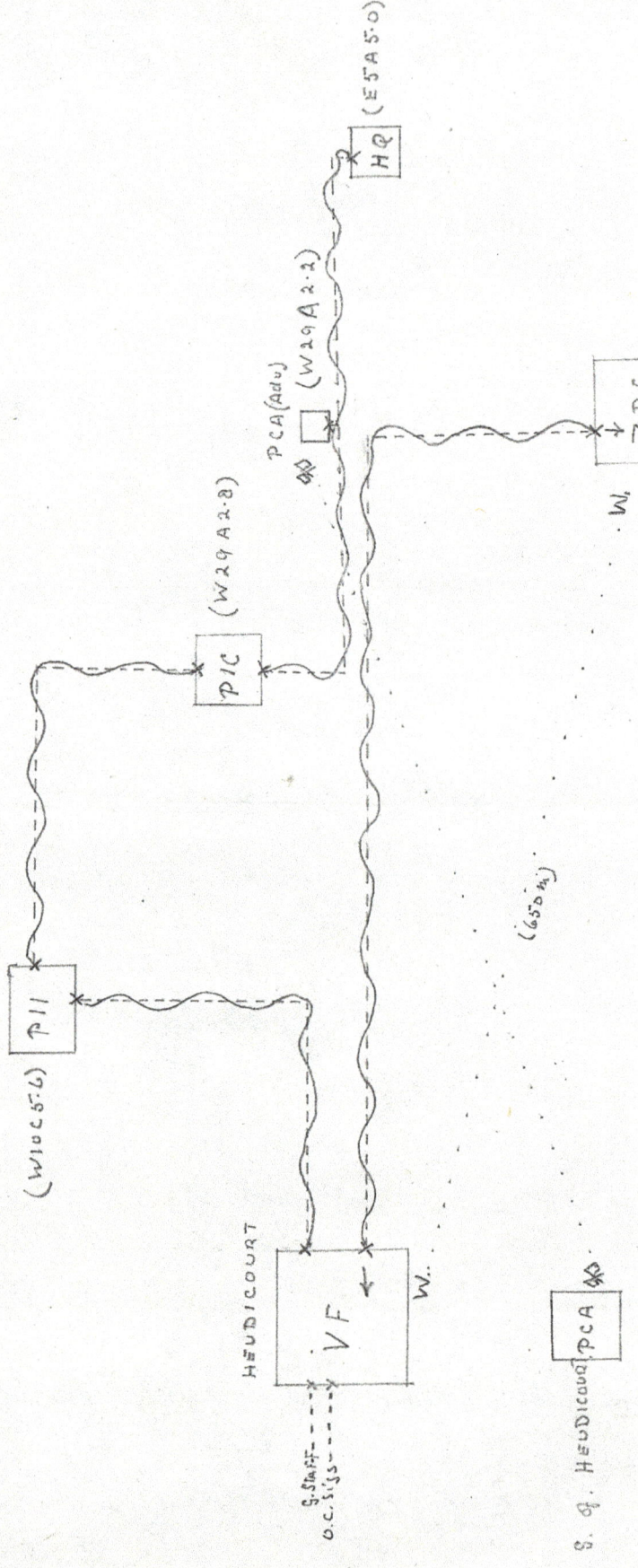

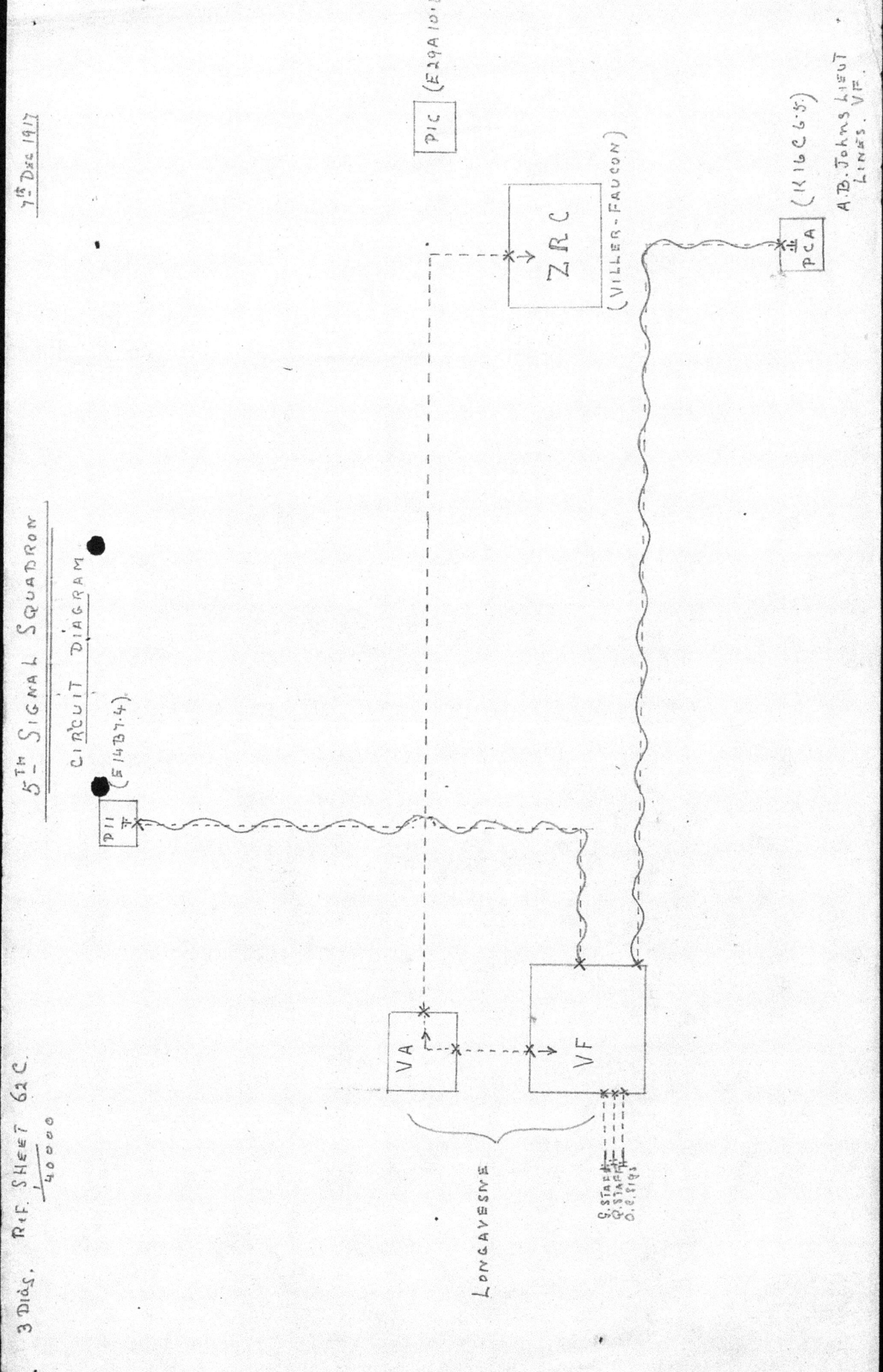

5TH SIGNAL SQUADRON
CIRCUIT DIAGRAM

[PCA] — ROISEL

[YX] — NOBESCOURT FARM

[PIC] CARTIGNY

[GCO] CATELET

[VF] MONCHY-LAGACHE
- 'G' STAFF
- 'Q' STAFF
- G.S.O.2
- COL. CAPPE
- O.C. SIGNALS
- PARCS
- S/L AIRCE
- FR. MISSION.

[ZCO] VILLERS-CARBONNEL

V.4.D.3.3. [P11]

10/12/17.
A. B. JOHNS. LIEUT.

23rd Dec 1917

5TH SIGNAL SQUADRON

CIRCUIT DIAGRAM

A.B. Johns Lieut
Lines. V.F.

Cav. Corps.

[ZCO]

Sub. Colm.

Can. Cav. Regt.

[PCA]

Dis. Div. Ord. Dump.

Ambala Cav Bde

[PIC]

[VF]
5th Cav. Div.

G.So. I
S. Staff
DA+QMG
OC. RE.
OC. Signals
DADOS
Hq. Mission
ADVS
A.T.O. Attach
ARI M.R.S.H
SIG M.R.S.H
M24 Mess

Field Squadron

[PII]

Secbad Bde

Army Form C. 2118.

WAR DIARY
OR
INTELLIGENCE SUMMARY.
(Erase heading not required.)

5TH SIGNAL SQUADRON

Month: **JANUARY 1918**

Place	Date	Hour	Summary of Events and Information	Remarks and references to Appendices
MONCHY LAGACHE	1/1/18		Division in reserve to Cavalry Corps. Communications as per diagram	Appendix 1
"	5/1/18		Orders received that Division would relieve 3rd Dismtd.	
"	10/1/18		Above orders cancelled. Officers signalling class started	
"	12/1/18		Information received regarding the move East of Indian regts. of 1st Division	
"	23/1/18		Warning Orders received from Division regarding relief of 1st Dismounted Division in the line	
"	24/1/18		Also Orders received for Division windmill store relief. Orders received regarding move of horses to DOMART area on completion of relief. Officers class broken up	
"	26/27-1-18		Relief of 3rd Dismounted Division by 5th Dismounted completed.	
BOUVINCOURT	27/1/18 10am		Bde. Headquarters & Staff took over from HQrs. Muffling Wing. 1st Bde. command of Dismtd. Division. Netherlands Canadian Bde. Reinforced by left MEREAUCOURT & marched to DOMART area	
"	28/1/18		1st Dismtd. Divn. relieved 2nd Dismtd. Division in the line	
"	30/1/18		Advance Rd. Rear Echelon left TERTRY marched to DOMART area. VF. closed at MONCHY LAGACHE at 12 noon & opened at DOMART same hour. 3rd Cav. Div Church took over at MONCHY LAGACHE from 3 VF.	
"	31/1/18		Communications as per diagram	Appendix 2

A. Clay Grove Capt.
OC 5th Signal Squadron

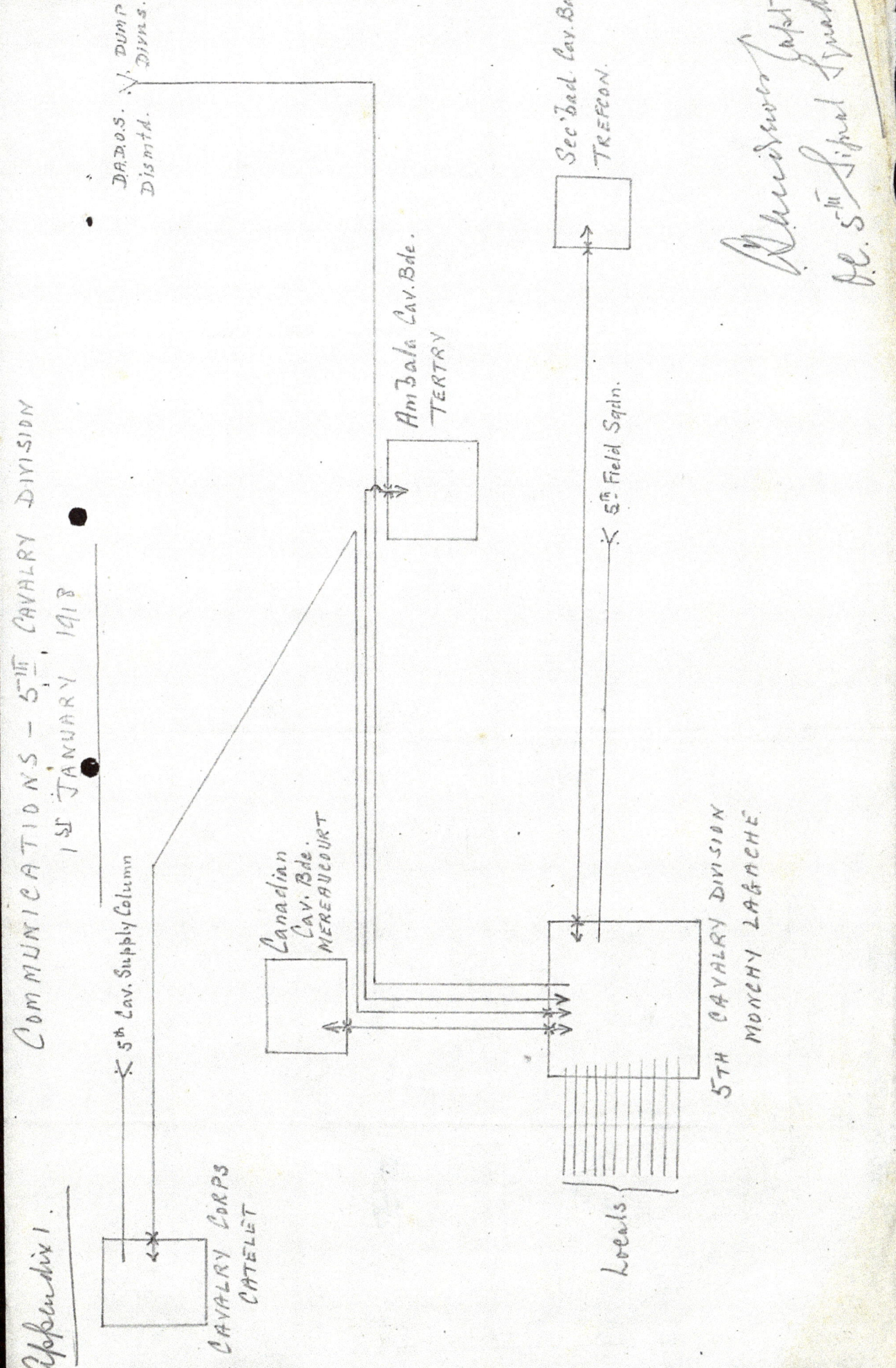

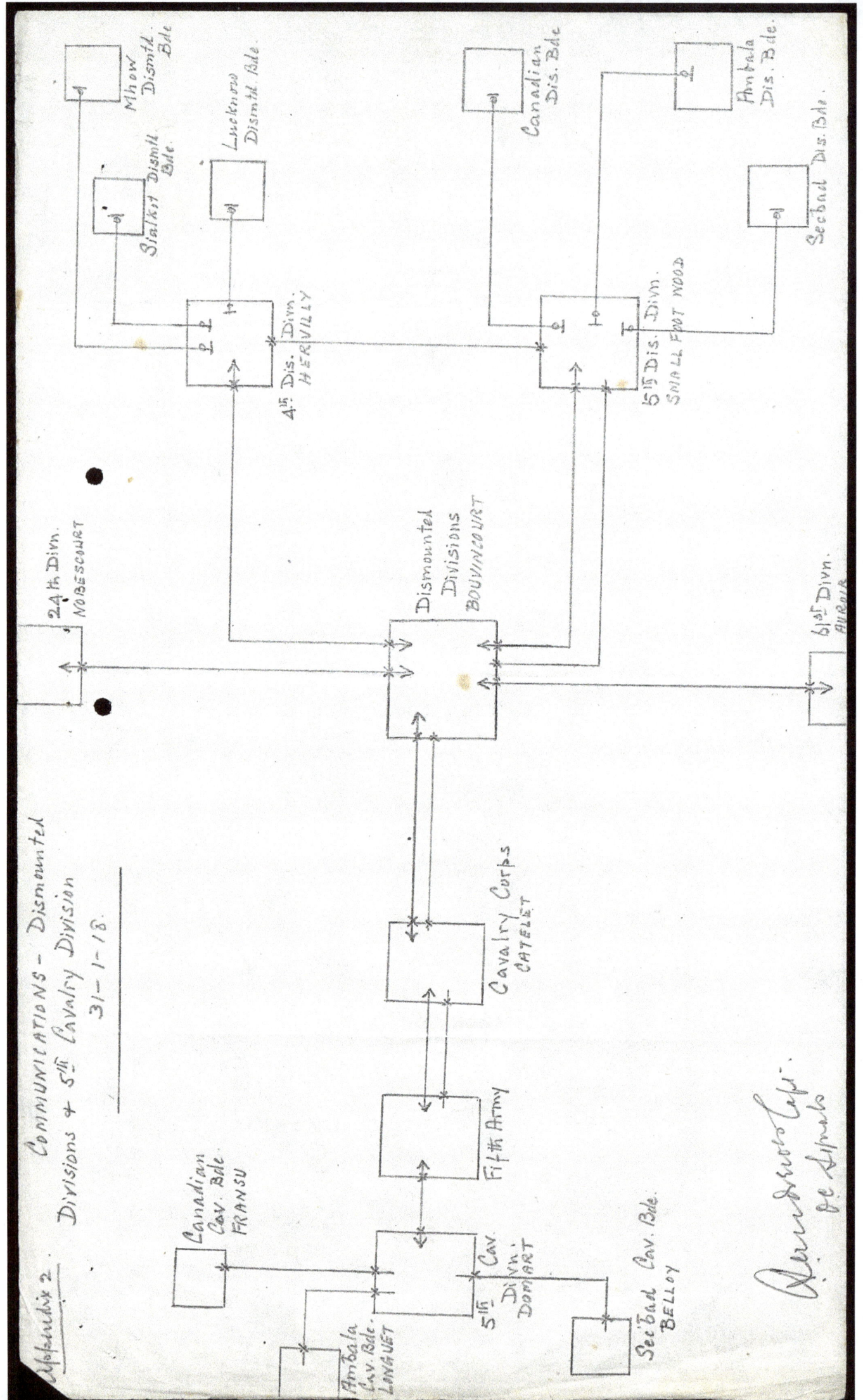

Army Form C. 2118.

WAR DIARY or INTELLIGENCE SUMMARY.

February 1918.   5th Signal Squadron

(Erase heading not required.)

Instructions regarding War Diaries and Intelligence Summaries are contained in F. S. Regs., Part II. and the Staff Manual respectively. Title pages will be prepared in manuscript.

Place	Date	Hour	Summary of Events and Information	Remarks and references to Appendices
BOUVINCOURT	1-2-18		4th & 5th Dismounted Divisions in the line. 5th Signal Sqdn in charge of signals dismounted divisional area. (V2)	
	7-2-18		Route diagram of area completed	
	11-2-18		Pole diagram of area completed	
	13-2-18		Received preliminary orders regarding relief	
	15-2-18		Squadron horses & transport marched from BOUVINCOURT to PONT de METZ	
			24th Div relieved 4th Dismounted Div in the line	
	16-2-18		5th Cav Div closed at DOMART at 9 am and marched to PONT de METZ	
	17-2-18		Gen. Mullins & Staff took over from Gen Kavanagh & left the command of Dismtd Divns	
PONT de METZ			5th Signal Sqn took over from 5th Signal Sqn. VF opened up at 10 am at PONT de METZ to Command with 2CD; 1/2; CCA, thro' and ex.	
			In comm. with CIC, PH thro' and ex.	
	19-2-18		Thro' to VD by morse	
	21-2-18		Thro' to 2CD by morse	
	22-2-18		Units of 5th Cav Div started to entrain for transfers	

Alan [signature]
Lt
OC 5th Signal Sqn

Army Form C. 2118.

WAR DIARY
or
INTELLIGENCE SUMMARY

(Erase heading not required.)

For MARCH 1918 5th Signal Squadron

Hour, Date, Place	Summary of Events and Information	Remarks and references to Appendices
PONT du METZ. March 1st – 2nd. March 8th. March 20th. MARSEILLES. March 30.	Comms as on 28th February. Mounted men transport entrained for Marseilles. Dismounted men entrained for Marseilles. 5th Signal Squadron embarked on H.T. "MENOMINEE" In Egypt.	

www.ingramcontent.com/pod-product-compliance
Lightning Source LLC
Chambersburg PA
CBHW081554160426
43191CB00011B/1925